ABOUT THE AUTHOR

Lars Muhl was born in Aarhus in 1950. He attended The Royal Academy of Music, Aarhus (Det Jyske Musik-konservatorium) from 1974 to 1976. For many years, he was a successful singer-songwriter – first as a band member, and then from 1986 as a solo artist. In 1996, he was awarded the WCM's Songwriters Million Certificate.

The author has had a great interest in spirituality from a very young age, and, concurrently with his music, he studied the world's religions and esoteric knowledge. Then, in 1996, he was struck down by an unexplained illness, which neither doctors nor alternative therapists could diagnose. This was the start of a completely new existence and the beginning of that quest he has so grippingly described in *The Seer*. In 1999 Lars Muhl decided to leave music to concentrate fully on his spiritual interests.

Lars Muhl has studied Aramaic, the language of Jesus, and has spent many years writing and lecturing on spirituality throughout the world. In 2003 he started Hearts and Hands, a non-profit and apolitical aid organization based on the voluntary work of various therapists. The aim is to help people who are suffering from life crises such as cancer and stress-related illnesses. In 2009 Lars Muhl and his wife Githa Ben-David founded the Gilalai Institute for Energy and Consciousness.

THE
MAGDALENE

VOLUME 2 OF THE ⊙ MANUSCRIPT

LARS MUHL

WATKINS
Sharing Wisdom Since
1893

This edition first published in the UK and USA 2017 by
Watkins, an imprint of Watkins Media Limited
19 Cecil Court
London WC2N 4EZ

enquiries@watkinspublishing.com

Design and typography copyright © Watkins Media Limited 2017

Text copyright © Lars Muhl 2017

1 3 5 7 9 10 8 6 4 2

Designed and typeset by Donald Sommerville

Printed and bound in Finland

A CIP record for this book is available from the British Library

ISBN: 978-1-78678-047-8

www.watkinspublishing.com

'I and my bride are one, just as Mariam the Magdalene –
whom I have chosen and sanctified as an example –
is one with me.'

Yeshua, *The Gospel of The Nazarenes*

Prologue

The train started with a jerk. I opened the parcel. It contained a manuscript almost 400 pages long. The main title was *Kansbar, the Protector of the Grail* and underneath the subtitle *Alhambra 1001*. Then a small introduction:

'Kansbar is not my real name. But due to the secrets I have been chosen to guard, I have taken this old Persian name. Kansbar the Chosen One. Kansbar the Wise. Kansbar the Seer. Kansbar the Protector of the Grail. I am getting old. For many years I have been searching for the one who is to take over this duty after me – but in vain. Only now do I remember the day I met Flegetanis, an itinerant Moorish singer, in a marketplace in a small town on the coast of Andalusia. This manuscript is for him. This is the story of the Grail.'

Back in Denmark I immediately started to write the manuscript which later became the book *The Andalusian Seer.*

I was so occupied with this task for the first few months that I forgot all about the old Andalusian manuscript which the Seer had left in my care. If the sun one day hadn't shone its rays onto my bookcase and pointed to the manuscript with an insisting finger, it is hard to say how long it might have stayed there collecting dust. Now I took it, opened it with a pounding heart and started to read:

'There once was a king's daughter who came from far away, and no one knew whence she had come but they saw that she was unique, beautiful and wise in everything she did, and they were astonished when they saw that she was surrounded by 32 rays of golden light. They said, "She is truly born of the light since the world is enlightened through her deeds." They asked her, "Where do you come from?" She answered, "From my own place." They said, "Then your people must be blessed. Blessed be you and blessed be your place." She said, "Let those who desire this blessing follow me. I have come to establish true balance in the world." But most of them hesitated for they had no faith in a woman. Not until she had disappeared and no longer enlightened the world did they repent and look for her, but in vain. Then they visited the wisest man in the country and asked him, "What are those 32 rays of golden light?" He answered, "Those 32 rays are paths. They each represent the king in the innermost chamber of his palace, and the number of chambers was 32, and there was a path leading to each of the chambers." The wise man was further questioned: "Did the king allow anyone access to his chambers along those paths?" No! Did he allow his pearls, his hidden treasures and his divine things be shown? No! What did the king do? He took his daughter and collected all the paths in her and her gown, and anyone who desired to set foot in the innermost chamber had to see her. The king in his endless love for her called her "my daughter" for she was his daughter. At other times he called her "my mother" or "my sister" but at all times he called her "my beloved one".'

1

It had been raining all that Sunday and also throughout the night. It was as if the floodgates of the Flood itself had been opened. I was in my study lost in the endless rain and the soaked landscape outside. The air was tense with static electricity. Something indefinable was gathering across the sea, a series of dark shadows of breaking clouds filled with unanswered questions.

I had just finished the manuscript for *The Seer*, when the phone rang.

'Now is the time,' a familiar voice stated.

It was the Seer.

'Meet me at Montségur, Friday next week.'

I wanted to say something but the words got stuck in my throat. A deep, warm sense of happiness flowed through me. Maybe I had given up on hearing from him again. He had been in my dreams and I had experienced the presence of his inspiring power from afar. What else could I want? Now I was sitting here afraid that he would disappear from my life again.

'Be vigilant,' he said, 'it is close to quarter day.'

The connection was cut off and I was left with the world's loneliest note in my ear. Quarter day? What was all that about? Was it just another example of the Seer's well-known sense of drama or his equally precise sense of timing?

The mere sound of his voice once more activated the invisible language with which I was slowly becoming familiar and which I was aware was only used when something unavoidable was to be communicated: a sound which could be received only by one who had been initiated into it. The ominous and no-nonsense undertone was unable to dampen my joy at having heard from him again.

'*See. Wake up and SEE!*' a voice whispered.

On the following day a catastrophe struck which was to change the sense of reality for a whole generation on several continents. The day was 11 September 2001 – the day that the Tower of Babel, the Twin Towers, came crashing down. The generation was called fear and the part of the world was the Western World.

Quarter day!

It was a rude awakening. Finally the abscess burst and we now stood paralysed, staring blindly into our own self-made darkness. But instead of a willingness to see, the leaders of the world once more chose the destructive escape route of repression and fear: projection – the hopeless result of a one-sided, rigid and masculine desire for power.

'*Only immature leaders need external enemies,*' a voice whispered.

I couldn't help think what the world would look like if the

2

Tibetan Buddhist monasteries in India, the Greek Orthodox monasteries of Mount Athos in Greece, Medjugorje in Bosnia, Manitou in Crestone, Colorado, the spiritual descendants of Black Elk in the Black Mountains and the Seer's office in Andalusia, did not work intensively to uphold the paper-thin balance between earthly insanity and a universal order in co-operation with the higher powers. Where would we be?

Everything surges with a deep sense of pain in this time and age. It is the old used-up powers turning and twisting in their death throes in a last, desperate attempt to maintain the status quo of their power. Deep beneath the ice cap of repression the earth and every soul is trembling in labour, foreshadowing that soon something new and long-awaited is about to be born, a cosmic power that people have not been able to recognize before because they are only now learning to open up to it. *Realization!*

In my childhood home we had one of these strange ornaments, which today we might call a hate-gift, a miniature, marble sundial with a plaque saying 'Do as I do – count the bright hours only'. One day while studying this small monument to the repressions of humanity, I suddenly thought to myself 'What are we going to do with all the dark hours?' It was not until I met the Seer and started working with him, that I understood that what we call darkness is only the hidden qualities waiting to be illuminated and activated.

'I'm glad I live in a country like Denmark,' the taxi driver said just as we arrived at the Aarhus Central Station, 'something like that could never happen here.'

I nodded in agreement, mainly to be polite and paid for the trip. The sky was leaden and closed. There was a sleepy, trance-like bustle in the arrival hall. Next to the news about 'Islam's Attack on the West' on the front page of a newspaper,

I saw a headline saying, 'Sales of Prozac Explode'. In a dark corner smelling of urine a number of flies circled around a huddled, dirty bundle, which I assumed was a human being.

Somewhere inside me a landscape was becoming more and more visible. Sometimes it showed itself as a large meadow with a foggy, milk-like horizon which had no beginning and no end. No people were to be seen. The cry of a raven cut the air as if it wanted to announce the ensuing silence, which made everything vibrate in what I could only describe as an ominous emptiness. Maybe it was our most basic and most feared state of life, the loneliness, which thus manifested itself as an inner, endless and surreal setting like a bridge between perdition and transformation. Perhaps it was the beginning of a nightmare or a new life. The choice was up to the lonely one – a choice which had to be made well every day, every second.

Everything had changed since I got home from Andalusia and the Seer. As I gave up my old worries and practised the difficult art of *being*, I started a whole new life.

A voice was coming alive: '*You are a leaf in the wind; a leaf falling through the air and landing exactly where it belongs, not haphazardly but unpredictably. You are a leaf in the wind. But you are also the wind. The leaf is transient. The wind is eternal.*'

In the same way I was the urine-smelling bundle in the darkest corner of the railway station. But I was also the one who passed him by. I convinced myself that it was not a lack of compassion. No. I recognized a brother in an impossible situation. But I also knew that somehow it was also an illusion, and that it was neither meaningless nor without hope, but rather the most certain possibility of change. It was a confrontation with all my rigid ideas about humanity's deepest obligation: helping a fellow human being in need. I had the understanding that the apparent arrogance in such a way of thinking might really be the first step towards a deeper appreciation of the word respect. This was a key to the simple lecture from that Voice about being a leaf in the wind. On the other hand it was also a challenge to move into the unknown darkness, where only the most hopeless beings wander restlessly about, in order to see that those beings are really hidden aspects of ourselves *being the wind that carries the leaf through the air.*

From the moment I put pen to paper it was like getting on a train that thundered into a tunnel where time ceased to be, not going backwards nor forwards, but into the present in which I was writing.

Everything I had learned thus became an unlimited reality. Writing was in itself an act of expansion of consciousness. A transformation of consciousness through which I finally, although carefully, might confirm the magic words: *I make myself available. I accept my responsibility.*

While I was writing *The Seer*, something else occurred which marked a final shift in my apparently insoluble financial problems. It happened on the day when an enticing voice tried to lure me into taking a tailor-made role as a seedy pop-singer in the TV series *The Hotel*. Was this the answer to my financial problems or the final temptation? Suddenly I knew. I knew that if I accepted the offer it would just be a backward step to all that I had tried to free myself from. I politely declined. I declined the enticing salary, which might have saved my frail finances, but couldn't give me the new life I so desperately yearned for. I said no to the seedy pop-singer who did not exist any more. Just like that! In exactly that moment another door opened. A debt I had paid several times because of the compound interest was suddenly waived. Unexpected offers of lectures arrived by mail. Zap!

How was this possible?

Could the answer be that I had given up nurturing the problems with my worries? Could the reason be that, finally, I showed some confidence in that which really mattered, the *métier* that was mine? Was this the visible result of following the Seer's simple teaching about stepping into the flow? Maybe the Board upstairs had not given up on me yet?

The train slid silently into the bleak landscape. I was looking at the fields and the trees, which continuously disappeared and reappeared. The window misted up a little and in its fog-like reflection I thought that I could discern a vaguely familiar face. At first I thought it was my own reflection, but then I saw that it belonged to a much older man. A woman appeared behind this face. I turned around.

'New passengers?'

The conductress smiled. Slightly confused, I found my ticket and gave it to her.

'Foix – isn't that the town of the Virgin?' she said casually, the way she might have commented on the weather. It was more of a statement than an actual question.

She punched my ticket and gave it back to me without waiting for an answer.

Did I hear correctly?

'Excuse me,' I said rather confused, 'what did you say?'

'Have a pleasant journey,' she said smiling with a raised voice as if talking to a deaf person. She disappeared down the aisle.

I changed trains in Hamburg and again in Cologne.

Twenty-five kilometres outside Paris, the train stopped in the dark. Panic spread throughout the train. Bomb threat. Shortly afterwards, we were told to leave our seats and go outside. Serious faces. A child cried inconsolably. In the carriage where I was sitting, they had stopped glancing secretively at an Arabian-looking man – now they stared directly and accusingly at him. I froze to the core of my being.

An hour later we were on our way again. The delay meant that we just missed being caught in an explosion on the outskirts of Toulouse. A fertilizer factory had been the target of terrorism – or maybe it was just one of those accidents that will happen. An hour after the explosion we slowly moved through a charred suburb filled with crumpled cars, melted street lamps and houses without windows. It was like travelling on the edge of a volcano.

The Seer met me at the station in Foix. He seemed taciturn and distant. Only the patriarchal aura around him gave its familiar glow to the surroundings. We pushed our way through the throng of people. The Seer's car was parked outside.

We didn't talk. Instead I watched the mountains as we drove through the pass onto the plateau leading to the village. After half an hour's driving I could see the mountain of Montségur between the trees. I felt something warm flowing through me. Deep inside I sensed something indefinable loosening up. We passed the mountain and descended round the hairpin bends towards the village. The house was right in front of me and, seeing it, I realized how much I had missed it.

'What do you want here?'

In spite of the fact that I knew his style pretty well by now, I was still taken aback. He took a large pitcher and poured water into two glasses with pastis in them. Then I heard myself saying:

'You asked me to come. I was afraid that I should never hear from you again.'

He looked straight at me for the first time.

'Have you forgotten everything I taught you? Tell me, how on earth could it ever happen that you and I would lose each other? We, who have never been apart.'

He lifted his glass and touched mine. I sipped at mine. I didn't like it. Inside me the foreign voice continued the sentence, which had been cut short:

'What you experience as separation is yet another escape into the illusion which believes in dividedness. From this another disease grows: longing.'

What did I long for?

'Tell me, do you think it was me who asked you to come? Do you think it was you who heard it and obeyed? Or could you imagine that such a way of thinking was just an expression of your limited understanding of the beautiful confirmation, that you and I are one?'

He emptied his glass and poured more water before continuing:

'But if I repeat it enough times I suppose you'll end up understanding.'

He seemed distracted. Once more the mystical voice continued to speak:

'Only the one who is sleeping knows the surprise in waking up. And now that we are on the subject, which shadow of yourself allowed itself to be so arrogantly led astray by his own laziness thus leaving a brother in need at the Central Station in Aarhus?'

What kind of voice was this, where did it come from and why was it so insistent right now?

My confusion was not helped by the fact that the Seer didn't seem to be himself. He seemed strangely excited and frantically poured more pastis into his glass.

'I plan to break the autocracy of the Church and Christianity. It has outlived itself and is a limitation which has been in power far too long.'

He was sincerely indignant. I had no doubt that this was something that meant a lot to him. It was not the first time he had touched on this subject.

'If people knew what kind of lie they have been sold, they would abolish the Church right away. If I told you that Yeshua was a peasant boy who knew nothing and couldn't do anything, what would you say?'

His voice sounded sharp. I wondered whether this was another test, or whether he really meant it. There was nothing new in his statement. Anyone with the slightest knowledge of the real history behind the making of the New Testament would know that part of its contents should be taken with quite a large pinch of salt. Not just because of the obvious corrections which clearly had been made, but also in the light of all the new findings of the scrolls which saw the light in Qumran at the Dead Sea and Nag Hammadi in Upper Egypt about fifty years ago. This being said, there are scripture passages in the New Testament that are, to my mind, simple and irrefutably true whose secrets only a few Christian churches are aware of.

'Yeshua was nothing,' he repeated harshly, 'he was manipulated and used in the struggle for power. It was the apostles who ran the show.'

I didn't necessarily disagree with him on this latter part, but I felt that I had to protest against his statements about Yeshua. At a deeper level I knew that the Seer's ability to see at this moment was decided by his own personal opinion, which again had something to do with his past, an earlier life. This wasn't something I reached by way of a mental process, it was pure certainty. Within this certainty, Yeshua was not only the son of the Power (God), as the gospels said, but also a role model for all of us, his brothers and sisters. Exactly like the multitude of wise men and women filling our history.

At that moment I realized that this subject from then on would be a stumbling-block between us. And this fact, together with the indignation sounding from his words, filled me with a very deep feeling of loneliness, which made me sad. Also, there didn't seem to be any mediating factor which could loosen the conflict looming ahead of us.

'Remember,' the voice said within my chest, 'the energy follows the thought.'

I wanted to say something but there was no sound. There was nothing else to say. I felt that something was brewing. Something was about to open up. The Seer was bustling about with his boots in the hall. I was sitting in the kitchen lost in the silence and sensing that the air was active with creatures, momentarily showing themselves as sparks, as fire, jumping about in the pulsating light. I closed my eyes and slipped into another state of being. At that moment it became clear that this condition reached much further than the reality we experience with our normal senses. It is very difficult to explain and explaining is itself the greatest limitation. In this state there are no pictures, no ideas, by which the state may be communicated. There was no doubt that this was the beginning of a new chapter, not just in my spiritual upbringing, but also in the subject, for better or for worse, of trying to be a human being with a task to fulfil here on earth. The voice spoke to me from my inner core:

'It is important that you realize what kind of change is coming. It will turn all that you previously took for granted and considered to be true, upside down. Humanity's limited imagination, all its thoughts and ideas, all the fear and anxiety causing energies to be imprisoned within illusions, materialism and misunderstood religion, have created more anger and bitterness than they have created love and forgiveness. The kind of religion that men and women have created is usually a limitation of the eternal. Fear

10

keeps people in a state where they may be controlled. Once, it may have been necessary and in many ways even beautiful. However, the time has come for the energies to be set free. If humanity understood the concept of trust and the power it represents, it would have no need to limit reality.'

The voice softly fused into the silence, turning into small particles of light dancing out from my heart. My body told me that this was true.

'When you give in to fear you are doing the exact opposite of what you have come to do, which is changing matter into spirit, darkness into light, demons into useful possibilities. Any lie eventually turns into a ghost or a demon. And this is exactly what the Church has made out of the message. Whether the lie is born in the unconscious or in ignorance, it is still a lie. No one is to blame. It is not a kind of sin. It is more a sad fact but luckily a fact which may be changed. Do not take this as an opportunity to make more enemies. We have enough of those. Transform and set free. You may experience the journey you are about to take as a journey through yet more pictures and apparently new illusions. But imagine that the contents of the cauldron, which at the dawn of time was placed over the fire, become smaller by the second, because all the slag is burned away and only the purest and the simplest necessities remain – then you will begin to understand what is being talked about. And when even the picture is burning and both the cauldron and the fire do not exist any more, neither physically nor as an idea, when even the idea of empty space and the great silence is gone, then all is one in the One.'

It was as if the words turned the silence inside out and it seeped into the walls, which lost their solidity and opened outwards in waves – or maybe they opened inwards?

When finally I let go of the picture and opened my eyes, the candle in front of me had burned down and the smoke from it tickled my nostrils. A strange paradoxical feeling of rebellion and gratitude flowed through me. Everything the voice had said struck my own basic tone so clearly that all my previous ideas of what love was were reduced to what it was – a limp copy of a unique masterpiece. And this masterpiece manifested itself in the Voice:

'When humanity realizes that it cannot go on exclusively identifying love with emotions and sensations, and sees that love is much more than that, then people are given a new kind of flexibility. Emotions alone are far too unstable to build on. This doesn't mean that you should make yourself insensitive, but simply that you should set your feelings free. It means awakening to reality and starting to see. There are more and more so-called clairvoyant people advertising and swindling just because they are able to look into the sub-astral mess. But that doesn't move anything and has got nothing to do with real freedom. Instead, humanity is caught up in new ideas and illusions that form the basis for new churches, hierarchies and careers, which become a repetition of the old and well-known institutions which were the cause of your wish to be free to begin with. One doesn't make the lie less of a lie by calling it the truth. A dirty mind doesn't become clean by putting on a clean coat. Words are easy. Attitude and action mean change. The responsibility for yourself is yours and yours alone. No sage or seer can take it upon themselves. There are no shortcuts to Paradise. And all roads lead through what limited man sees as hell. That is why people do not want to take it upon themselves but project it onto a guru, another human being or their surroundings. When it comes down to it, there may be only one out of a million who really has the courage to free himself and take on responsibility for himself.'

I got up and walked over to the window but the voice continued:

'"Arise, take up your bed and walk – you are healed," someone once said. He might as well have said, "Arise and be responsible for yourself." It is now you yourself who changes things. It is now you yourself who must wake up and do what you have come to do. No more and no less. This is the option given to all people, right now!'

The particles of dust danced in a sunbeam falling through a kitchen window. The sound of the bells from the sheep on their way to the field at the other side of the road was a signal that the lesson was over. I went to my room to unpack and to get ready for the reunion with the mountain – my beloved Montségur.

It was a clear sky, the light was sharp and the air clean and pure as we walked through the thicket towards the female guardian of nature, Prat's meadow. Whispering beings danced around us for every step we took, and I had the sensation that they came alive because of the Seer and were busy welcoming us. Oddly enough, it didn't strike me as strange that such a sight now seemed quite natural. Maybe because it hadn't dawned on me yet that in the words of the Voice this was a step into a new sphere that had not yet settled in my consciousness, and I was once more satisfied with the fascination itself and not the symbolic content behind it.

Prat was expecting us. The Seer and I walked side by side and it felt as if we were drawing all the vertical and horizontal lines after us into the centrifugal force which was prevalent at this place, until they formed an equilateral, rotating cross, which was centred here and offered to our beautiful friend by invisible hands.

I saw her faintly in the empty square, her transparent, graceful movements and embracing, radiating nature, hovering and vibrating in the air in front of us. I took one step aside and stared into the melting pot of the sun, into the essence of fire – the eternal re-melting process of matter and form – into the flowing glass of billions of years, into the dying mastodon of pain and life – into the limited cleansing dance of shadows; all of it limiting, pathetic words, pictures and ideas only; all of it nothing but a monument to the transience of form. But also a beautiful memory of the seed and the earth, the mustard seed growing and growing until it finally shatters the frozen crystal of the heart. A galactic explosion of timeless visions, predictions and prophecies, which fell like a redeeming rain in an age-old consciousness at this moment.

'Lars!'

The voice was inside and outside. There was no distance. The figure in whom I recognized the Seer was only an empty shell. Within the glowing square I saw Prat and an unknown consciousness united in a smile full of warmth and compassion radiating towards me. I was just about to throw myself into the fire in order to let myself be destroyed, when I felt a hand on my shoulder shaking me gently, and the voice of the Seer reaching me from outside:

'Lars!'

We walked across the meadow. I followed him closely and thought that this was the reality he had talked so much about. It wasn't a dream.

We passed the steep and straight part with ease and stopped at the stone erected to commemorate the death of the Cathars at the stake of the Inquisition.

'Something decisive has happened.'

The Seer watched me closely as he continued:

'I've got permission to show you the hidden path to the fortress.'

He pointed sadly towards a white fence of thin undressed spruce stems blocking what had once been a path, but which was now overgrown and had almost disappeared under bushes and tall grasses. Boulders were lying helter-skelter between overturned trees that had once been part of a forest and had later crawled up along the side of the mountain where it now spread around it like the hair around the bald pate of a monk.

We sat down in the grass.

'We'll start tomorrow morning early. This is just the beginning. You must prepare yourself. Prepare yourself to be one hundred per cent present. This is a chance that you may never get again. If you do this, you can do anything.'

I nodded without hearing what he was saying, but I simply got lost in the aftermath of all the fantastic experiences I had just had, content in the thought that now I could see. Momentarily, I was smitten by the disease that is a basic challenge in any kind of spiritual work: *vanity* – and I must have looked rather like a blithering idiot.

I do not know how long this lasted. Maybe it was the handful of sparrows hopping about in the grass that woke me up. I straightened my back, and inside me someone else was straightening his back. One who got up and took up his bed and got ready to walk.

'Well, now you have tried this also.'

The Seer was gentle and full of understanding:

'It is one of the children's diseases that you must get over in a hurry.'

The sun was on its way down behind the mountains, leaving a soft, pink hue swaddling the village and rendering a surrealistic gleam to the houses. The smell of sheep and pressed grapes mixed with the smell of burnt hawthorn coming from the village chimneys. A flight of white doves swung across the roofs like a live cloud and settled at the pigeon-loft where they belonged. We sat in the garden enjoying the last few minutes of twilight. Then the cold crept up from the ground and it was time to go back inside.

The Seer was cooking while I was setting the table in the banqueting hall and lighting a fire in the open fireplace. We found ourselves in a place other than the one we knew, maybe on another planet in another universe. I don't know what – only that we were on a journey of change through eternity.

While I was lighting the candles it struck me that the words of the Seer, when he called me, turned out to be true in every way. I now had no more doubts about what he meant by the word 'quarter day'. The journey from Aarhus to Montségur had been a journey from one kind of reality to another. Almost without participating myself, I had been guided through a transformation so radical that I was just beginning to understand that the lesson for the day was about giving up the most steadfast kind of resistance – *my own!*

I was slowly beginning to understand that the distance from one reality to the next as well as the shift between them could happen as easily as snapping my fingers; that the invisible basic steps in the cosmic dance could revoke every lead-filled step in the gravitational dance of death with no effort at all – if only you knew the score.

However, had I known what lay ahead, I would not have been as self-satisfied and confident.

After dinner I cleared the table and did the dishes. In the banqueting hall I saw the Seer lost in deep thought and staring into the fire. I was about to sit down when he turned towards me:

'Tonight you'll sleep at the Costes.'

The words fell quietly and precisely.

'I have booked a room for you.'

I was about to argue the point, but it was clear that this was not a subject for debate.

'We'll meet here tomorrow at 7 a.m.'

'Is something wrong?'

He shook his head:

'No, this is just the way it must be.'

'Have I done anything wrong?'

'Just go – tomorrow you'll know why.'

He walked towards the staircase leading upstairs:

'Good night.'

In the gleam from the open fire reflecting its light in the glass door I saw a shadow of an unfamiliar being which seemed to smile laconically and almost fatalistically. I cannot say for sure, but it seemed as if the features were jackal-like. From far away I heard my own voice answering him:

'Good night.'

2

She was twelve years old when, for the first time, she saw the man that her parents had promised her to. It was just a glimpse. She saw him from a balcony at her parent's palace in Bethany. He was received in the courtyard by the servants who washed the dirt from the traveller's feet as was the custom in this country. She shivered from excitement at the sight of this handsome young man, eighteen years of age, whom she had heard so much about. The excitement spread to her small breasts and made the blood rise in her cheeks and quickened her breath.

This was *her* great day. She was now a fully matured woman who was able to love a man and to give birth to his children. She wanted most of all and right away to throw her arms around his neck, but she knew that she had to be patient and that she would probably have to wait for a year, at the most two years, before her dream would come true. This was not a regular wedding. Much more was at stake than the whimsical love of a young girl. The whole nation nourished the hope that from this occasion, once and for all, the age-old wound would be healed, that the dismembered people would be whole again and that Israel once more would become an autonomous nation beyond the reaches of Roman tyranny. And all of this depended upon the union between the tribes of Benjamin and Judah.

One of her two older sisters, Martha, together with a maid, helped her to get ready for the engagement party. They teased her in their playfulness by exaggerating their movements when washing her in the most intimate places, while they giggled and told her about all the terrible things a man would do to a woman when finally she belonged to him.

There were already rumours about her amazing beauty. Rumour had it that, without any doubt, she would develop into the most beautiful woman Jerusalem had ever nurtured. Hope-filled wooers had asked her parents for her hand in marriage, but all of them had been forced to leave the palace without having accomplished their object. Even Teutilus, a mighty Roman merchant and a close friend of Herod Antipas, had thrown out a feeler. This had caused a great uproar among the Jews, who had expressed their anger over such an insult quite unreservedly. Who did he think he was? Not only was he a Roman, he was also a very old man. This was a violation of all rules – written as well as unwritten.

After a week, however, the anger had died down and Teutilus instead became the butt of Jerusalem's most biting sarcasm. The man had simply made a fool of himself.

Her father, Zerah, had calmly and quietly refused any offer. He was from Benjamin's tribe but grew up in exile in Egypt just like Moses. Later, he had served under a Syrian king and had been rewarded with property in Jerusalem and Bethany.

He and his wife, Jezebel, who came from a wealthy family from the tribe of Dan, were close acquaintances of the groom's family and both families regarded the coming union as a fulfilment of the oldest prophecies. The expectations originating in these had their roots far back in a time before Abraham. This was not just an important, political wedding. This was a religious merging blessed by YHVH himself.

When the two women had finished washing the young girl, they anointed her with fragrant balms. The dress was traditional and consisted of a long, white slip followed by a red tunic edged with golden threads reaching to her knees. As tradition demanded from any Syrian virgin, a pale blue *chiton* was placed over it, long enough to touch the floor. It was edged with small, golden flowers, was modestly closed at the side, and a veil was sewn on to it. They finished dressing her by placing the same tiara on her head which her mother and her mother's mother-in-law had worn at their engagement festivities before her, and which would be given to her on the day of her wedding.

She spun around laughing so that the women could see the result of their efforts. They clapped their hands in excitement and surrendered to the girl's catching laughter. It was time to introduce the future bride and groom to each other.

They stood at either end of the most beautiful hall of the palace. He was surrounded by his mother, a brother and two teachers, and she by her mother, her older brother, the two sisters and a few maids. The distance between them was so great, that she could barely make out his face, but it seemed to her that he looked too sad for her liking, considering the occasion.

The invited guests were lining both sides of the hall, expectant and smiling, carrying gifts and waving at them with palm leaves. The two patriarchs, Zerah and Yoasaph, were standing in the middle of the hall exchanging traditional greetings and shaking hands as a sign of the coming pact.

It was a moving sight and some people cried since this was a moment that most Jews had been longing for. That which few people had dared to hope for was about to happen: the seed for the unification of Israel and the freedom of Israel had been planted – Israel – the chosen people of the Lord.

Disappointingly, that day she saw no more of her groom to be. Men and women dined separately. And although she could hear the loud talking of the men from the hall next door, this only enhanced her longing for him. After the meal they danced and sang, but this also was done in separation. Sooner than expected, the festivities were over and it was time to go to bed.

Two years passed very slowly. She did not meet her groom to be during that time, and when she asked about him she was told either that she shouldn't worry about it or she didn't get an answer at all. For the sake of the outside world, she tried to keep her dignity, but inside she grew more and more disconsolate.

To pass the time she accepted any kind of work she could be given. The servants tried to talk her out of it, but she begged them until they gave in and let her participate on equal terms with them. Each time it was discovered, it ended in embarrassing situations. She had to stand in front of her father, who with great resignation tried to make her understand what was suitable for a girl of her birth.

One day, however, when she was busy helping the washer-women in the wash-house, something happened that would turn everything upside down. As she was beating the water out of the clothes against the stones at the edge of the pond, she happened to look at the surface of the water. In a glimpse she saw something moving. At a closer look, however, there wasn't anything to be seen. This happened again a little later, but again there was nothing to be seen. She tried to ignore it, but it kept getting close to the surface of the water every time she looked away. Maybe she was over-worked? Maybe it was her monthly cycle weaving a spell over her?

She sat down on the edge of the pond in order to regain her composure. As she sat there, not focusing on the water, a picture became visible. She stared at it with rapt attention. It showed her mother and her father travelling with a caravan in a foreign part of the country. The picture made her smile. She recognized the extreme air of seriousness that her father always assumed whenever he wanted to say something disarming and funny. She was about to laugh out loud when the idyllic picture changed brutally. Foreign warriors and highway robbers attacked the peaceful caravan in an ambush. In a terrifying moment she saw a heathen slitting her father's throat from behind, while her mother was cut down mercilessly with a scimitar. Everything went red in that moment. She jumped up with a scream at the terrible sight, which made all the women drop whatever they had in their hands in order to come to her aid. Since they couldn't see anything they assumed that she didn't feel well and carried her to her room where they laid the inconsolable girl on her bed.

She stayed in bed for three days. Her sisters sat with her and they tried, without any luck, to make her tell them what had happened at the wash-house that had been so terrible. Knowing that they wouldn't understand, she refrained from telling them about her vision. Even when both her mother and father separately sat with her, she couldn't bring herself to tell them about it. The only one she knew would take her seriously was her brother, but he was in Jerusalem on private business.

She felt faint when her mother came to her that same afternoon beaming with joy, and told her that she and her father were going on a journey to Antioch in order to visit some relatives, and that the girls were very welcome to join them. They would start out immediately on the following day.

The mother got quite frightened when the girl threw herself into her arms and, sobbing, begged her to stay at home, that it was bad luck to make such a journey at this time, that she had seen something that no one could ever understand but which nevertheless was a fatal omen.

'But what have you seen?' the mother asked and stroked her hair.

But the ominous words wouldn't come forth. They stuck in her throat and nearly choked her.

'Please listen to me. You cannot possibly go.' she begged.

But the mother simply smiled at the daughter, touched by her compassion.

'All right. You may stay at home with Martha and Mari, then. They probably want to stay with you anyway.'

As soon as her mother had left she got out of bed, determined to go to Jerusalem to find her brother in order to tell him about it. If anyone might prevent their parents from going, he was the one. She knew that this was an insane plan and that there wouldn't be one single person in the palace who would help her make it come true. But the vision she had seen was so real to her that she did not doubt the authenticity of it for one moment.

She waited until dusk. With her face hidden behind a dark cape she moved like a shadow along the wall of the orchard to the rear of the palace. She succeeded in passing her father's bodyguard, one man guarding the west gate. She crept along behind the thickets until the road turned, and then stepped out on to the road to Jerusalem.

There were not many travellers to be seen, and the few she met didn't recognize her. The sun sank behind the horizon and the dust and the earth took on a fiery red tint. She felt a crushing grief in her heart but continued undaunted, determined to complete her task. A cloud of dust appeared. It looked like a lonely wanderer in the distance. For a moment she thought that someone was calling out her name. She stopped and, somewhat frightened, looked behind her. But no one was there. In front of her the cloud of dust approached. She stepped to the side of the road in order to avoid drawing attention to herself. She blinked and tried to see clearly. She had completely lost her sense of distance. The moment the sun disappeared she felt like turning back, but continued nevertheless. In front of her the road lay empty. The cloud of dust had disappeared.

'Mariam, Mariam, have you forgotten who you are?'

She froze at the sound of the voice and looked around in confusion, but she couldn't see anyone. Then she spotted a figure in the shadow of a bush at the side of the road. Frightened, she stepped back.

'Fear not Mariam, I am your protector.'

She could now faintly make out the face of the figure. It was an elderly woman with long, white hair.

'Who are you?' she asked in a quivering voice.

'You'll know soon enough who I am. For now, it suffices for you to know that I'm a friend. You must return to Bethany immediately. What must pass will come to pass.'

She looked into the dusk but all she saw was the bush moving softly in the wind. The figure had disappeared. For a moment she was in doubt, but then she regained her presence of mind, the presence of mind that the old woman's voice had conjured up. The state of confusion only appeared because she was caught between that which she felt she had to do for the wrong reasons and what she knew she had to do because it was written. She turned about and started walking back. In the distance she saw a Roman unit patrolling the roads.

She cried the next morning when her parents said goodbye before setting out on their journey to Antioch. When she threw herself into her father's arms she sensed a force holding her and the voice from the previous day saying:

'What must pass will come to pass.'

It was very strange how she accepted this assurance unquestioningly knowing that 'what must pass will come to pass' would be a catastrophe for her and her brother and two sisters. But how could anyone explain the power that she felt growing inside of her, in spite of her fears – a power filled with destiny and prophecy. She could scarcely understand this herself. Was she possessed by something evil?

'What must pass will come to pass.'

It was as if the heart was a book in which a new page was turned, a revelation of a totally new language, a certainty which was not thrown off course by the disastrous situation she was in, a kind of transfiguration looking directly through the veils into the essence of things at the centre of existence. And she saw her parents in their spiritual clothing, high above the corporeal state, smiling through her tears, which mixed with the dust and left small traces on her cheeks. She held them for a long time.

'What is the matter with you?' her father exclaimed and held her close.

'Nehwey sibyanak aykana d'shmeya aph b'arah?' he whispered in her ear.

At that moment she knew that he also knew. One question only burned in her heart. Why?

She stayed there with Martha and Mari and the servants until they lost sight of the caravan, then she broke down and cried knowing that she had seen her parents alive for the last time.

The fatal news reached Bethany two weeks later. It was her brother Lazarus who brought the message of death to Jerusalem where as the new head of the family, he had received the sad tidings via two surviving soldiers from his father's bodyguard. The rumour of his little sister's vision had also reached him, but he had shaken it off as if it was some kind of contagious disease or an evil mirage. But the maltreated bodies of his parents that the soldiers brought with them were very real, and Lazarus had to acknowledge that all this had happened just like his sister had seen and predicted.

Due to the condition of the bodies he had to refrain from the traditional burial ritual. The embalming had an almost ritualistic character. The corpses had to go into the ground right away.

Only a small number of the closest relatives participated at the burial. She was trance-like during the whole ceremony and felt the presence of the white-haired woman she had met on the road to Jerusalem and in whom she had recognized the magnificent power that spoke to her. That woman's calm became her calm.

When Lazarus was about to go into the tomb with the bloody clothes and other items as tradition demanded, she calmly stepped forward, took the clothes and the other things out of his hands and quietly walked into the burial chamber without anyone protesting. A decisive change had taken place in her. She was surrounded by an inexplicable authority and dignity that seemed quite natural but which normally wasn't accorded to a girl that young.

The tomb was cool. Only a narrow, dusty ray of light showed her the way. She could only see the two white bundles faintly on their designated places to the rear of the burial chamber. Taking the three steps down into the cold darkness she immediately felt his presence. In an attempt to stay calm she bowed down and carefully placed the items she had been carrying at the feet of the dead. Getting up again she stared directly into two burning eyes. At first she recognized the old woman. Then the face seemed to change and she recognized her fiancé. She put her hand out towards him but he gently waved her back and she heard him saying, '*Not yet.*'

She sensed that the air around her was filled with beings who wanted to help her, and they guided her as she stepped into the shaft of light. In the air in front of her a transparent, radiant and deeply purple ball hovered with a pink, four-pointed star within, surrounded by a thin, pink stripe.

'*This is your guardian angel,*' a voice announced. '*Follow it and you shall never go astray.*'

She stayed in the shaft of light and let herself be filled with the Power. Stepping out of the burial chamber, she carried the certainty of the radiant star in her heart and was surrounded by its deep pink and purple hue. At that moment the crying and lamentations of the women stopped. It was as if her mere presence transformed the curse of grief and gave a meaning to the moment, which they had never known before. At that moment Lazarus recognized her and saw who she really was.

Immediately after the burial of their parents Lazarus asked his little sister to meet him in their father's private room. In future he would be the one to rule from here. When she stepped into the room he was again surprised to see how much she suddenly seemed to be a stranger. He could recognize his sister, her by now legendary beauty, her burning eyes, her tall body with the promise of the magnificent shape of a rare and beautiful woman. But it seemed as if the direct, female vitality and playful air had been exchanged for a sweeter and more serious dignity that he hadn't noticed before. Something else, something radiant had taken over her being.

They embraced. He felt her small nipples through the thin material. He then held her at arms length and looked at her affectionately.

'If I didn't know better, I might think that you lusted after me,' she said laughing and blushed.

'The all compassionate God might have made that happen had I not been your brother,' he answered and pulled her head to his chest and continued:

'But a mightier goal has been set for you far more important than being given to a man solely for his dubious pleasures.'

'Are you forgetting that I have already been promised to someone?'

She tried to pull away from him and he hesitated but kept his grip around her waist. Then he said:

'No, I do not forget. How could I? But the groom appointed for you may not be the one you expect him to be.'

He spoke in a subdued voice. When she struggled to get free he let her go. She went silent. Although she had never spoken to her husband-to-be or had spoken to anyone about him or about the type of marriage she could expect, she had sensed from the beginning that it wasn't going to be a traditional marriage. Nevertheless, she was filled with the natural yearning of a young girl, and the picture of the one she was carrying in her heart was enough to light a secret fire in her body when she conjured it up. But she didn't know who he was.

Lazarus stayed by the window for a long time looking thoughtfully across the fields of grape without being able to speak. He was searching for the words but still hesitated. She sensed his perplexity. It suddenly struck her that maybe he knew more about her future husband than he wanted to admit.

'Do you know him?' she asked with newborn hope in her voice.

A sad smile crossed his face and a distant look came into his eyes. His voice was low and intense:

'It is said that he is destined to play a specific part.'

The sentence hung in the silence. They looked away from each other. He was wondering whether or not she was aware what this meant for her. She was considering the stranger.

'Who says this?' she asked.

'I heard it from the Essenes in a house in Jerusalem.'

'What specific part?'

'The Essenes are the kind of people who do not speak much.'

'What does he say himself?'

'Nothing.'

'Nothing? Hasn't he got anything to say?'

'He has gone away.'

She felt a stab in her heart.

'Where?'

Her voice was very small.

'First to Alexandria, then East.'

She turned and faced him. There were so many who gave themselves out to be special, the long-awaited Messiah for example. So many miracle-performers and prophets, who lit a fire in people and gave them false hopes of better times and eternal life.

'Is he like the horrible magician Hanina Ben Dosa?'

Her voice revealed that she didn't think much of the miracle-performer, whom they said could bring forth rain and many other things as he wished it. She had seen him once on a journey to Jerusalem with her father, Martha and Mari. They hadn't liked him. He seemed untrustworthy. Spoke too much, was smooth-tongued and made far too many exaggerated gestures. You could see his rotten teeth when he smiled. They had found him despicable. When she mentioned him now, in this connection, it was more an expression of her helplessness. Because she sensed that a curse and something fatal was hidden behind her brother's words, something that she didn't understand and wasn't sure if she was ready to fathom yet. Lazarus took her hands in his, looked affectionately at her and said:

'The time has come. It is about time you heard the truth.'

She felt a shiver running through her body and was about to say something, but he got in first and held a finger against her lips.

'Hush, sister! What I'm about to tell you is unavoidable. It is written and there is nothing we can do about it. You have also been chosen, just as he has. The time has come when you must accept your destiny. I shall tell you everything, but only on condition that you do not interrupt me. I do not want to make you sad, but you must promise me that you will stay and listen to what I have to say, no matter how much it may hurt you.'

He fell silent and pretended to give her time to think. But although with a part of her being she was terrified at the thought of the atrocities that were waiting behind the words he was about to say to her, she felt the new certainty deep in her innermost being filling her with a strength and lifting her above all the trivia of life. He began speaking:

'A great master is expected to come forward among the

Essenes. The long-expected Messiah. Your betrothed will play a great part in this connection. He may be the right hand of this great master. According to my source he is elected to be a high priest within the new order, which will make Israel a free nation once again.'

He fell silent – focusing on her reaction. She simply nodded.

'But even a high priest must have a wife. Do you understand what I'm saying?'

Again she nodded. Then she said:

'What you are saying is that this is a contract of marriage the sole purpose of which is to legitimize his function. A cover to make it possible for him to gain the trust of the people – isn't that true?'

He looked at her amazed. Her precise summing up of the situation took him by surprise.

'There is more,' he said. 'Nobody knows how long his preparations will take. Nobody knows when he will return. For the sake of all those involved it is better that you go to Those Dressed in White in the temple of Isis at Heliopolis to let them teach you. They will know how to prepare you for your task. The delta of the Nile will do you good. Our dear father would have approved this decision.'

His words made her want to scream. Instead she said:

'Which task?'

'Your task.'

'Who could know my task better than I do?'

She had a strong urge to go against him and all his limited ideas. But her reaction just made him shut her out.

'My mind is made up. You leave as soon as possible.'

The case was closed.

He turned his back on her and walked over to the window and stared into the void. At that moment she felt a deep compassion for him. Again she felt the strange presence of the loving Power and was conscious of the closeness of these benevolent beings. Did they come from him or the thoughts and desires he was holding, all that she felt he didn't dare confide to her – or all that he didn't dare look at himself. She went over and stood close to him, looking out of the window. The pictures passed her by in silence and she smiled when she saw the old white-haired woman disappearing in the vibrant cloud of dust in the air. Then she said:

'I know what you mean. I'll go and take upon me what is mine to do. What else is there to do? How could I do anything else? It is written. But tell me who are Those Dressed in White?'

Her words softened the tense atmosphere.

'The Society of the Brotherhood sprang from their midst. It was Those Dressed in White who founded the rules of conduct for the Essenes. They are also astrologers, prophets and healers. But they are much more than that. They are a kind of order of therapists that only a few know about. There is so much I would like to tell you, but I do not know enough about it. What is happening has been coming for a long time. If I could tell you more, I would.'

'Is he one of them?' she asked.

But her quiet, newly found certainty made the question seem both empty and meaningless. She had asked something to which she really knew the answer herself. And when she saw how her brother was nervously trying to keep his perspective and live up to his new dignity, she was sorry that she had asked the question. Finally he said:

'He has been brought up in the Brotherhood at the Mountain of Carmel. That is all I know.'

She put a finger on his lips.

'Say no more. It is written.'

3

Darkness was falling over the village as I walked through the narrow streets. The air was clear and cold. A dog was barking inside a house, and all around cats were busy catching mice. My thoughts moved in circles, trying to find a reason for the Seer's arrangement, but I didn't get any further than the question, why?

The light from the Hôtel Costes threw its cosy glow on to the street where the familiar white sign with black letters was hanging on the gable of the house welcoming travellers. I pushed the gate open and walked through the small garden. The owner, Gilbert, was busy arranging Cathar ornaments in the small glass case with souvenirs. Through the open door to the kitchen I got a glimpse of Gilbert's wife, Maurisette, who was busy cooking. One couple only waited for their dinner at one of the tables in the restaurant. A fly was circling around in the room. The radio was silent. It was late in the season.

Gilbert smiled knowingly when he spotted me as if we shared a secret and gave me a hearty welcome. I thought that he might have received a hint from the Seer about what was going on. But it made me happy that he recognized me at all. He pointed expressively at the bar, which was no more than a shelf with a few bottles behind the counter. I hesitated but then I asked for a glass of red wine and sat down in the front room. A little later he came back smiling widely and carrying two glasses and a bottle. He bore the latter proudly before him. It was Don César, one of the bottles that the Seer had brought with him from Spain as a present for Gilbert the last time we were in town. He poured wine into the glasses and we toasted each other. However, my poor French and Gilbert's non-existent English reduced all conversation to an inadequate mime-show. We gave up and limited our contact to the lifting of our glasses and drinking. I emptied my glass and got the key for room 1.

The room was situated on the first floor and had windows facing toward the garden: pale, flower-covered wallpaper, only a few pieces of furniture with a double bed in the middle of the room, a built-in wardrobe at one side and a small table at the foot of the bed. As I entered the room a cold wind swept past me and into the hall like an evil spirit out of a bottle. But I was under a kind of spell and didn't attach too much importance to it. Instead, I followed my intuition, walked over to the window, opened it and looked up at the nocturnal sky. At once I caught sight of a flickering light in the multitude of stars. At first I thought that it moved. But suddenly I saw that it was a star that was bigger than the others. I stood spellbound for a long time and couldn't leave this wonderful sight. I do not know how long I stood like this, but I came to, realizing that I was very cold. I closed the window, turned on the electric heater in the corner, lay down on the bed and slipped into a dreamless sleep.

I woke up when a flash of lightning pierced my stomach with an infernal sound and made me curl up in a foetal position on the bed, transfixed like a bug on a pin. The pain hit me directly at the centre. I screamed, but the sound was muffled by the noise. I was then thrown on to my back and kept there by a pipe-like shaft piercing my solar plexus. I just managed to think that this was it. But I didn't know what 'it' was. My last thought before disappearing was to call the Seer because I knew that this was more than I could possibly handle alone.

Then, before I could do anything, it started – relentlessly and without hesitation – like a train at full speed going through a tunnel – one picture after the other, pictures from my childhood, pictures from situations in my life, from earlier incarnations, pictures of being abandoned, alienation, a scoop in a small mud-filled bucket, old, red bricks from churchyards, monumental, closed, institution-like buildings, reformatories, military barracks and asylums; enormous, ill-fated, red and clumsy buildings on sunburned lawns, in dog-rose summers with buttermilk mucilage and buttermilk beards, without soft drinks and ice cream. Happy summers, newly fledged parents, blancmange and cherry sauce. Endless idyll. Buildings with locked doors, and windows that could only open slightly. Curfew in the dog-rose pointed sanctuary of long and hot afternoons, where transparent starched-nylon curtains did not move in the wind. *The Lucy Show* and *Perry Como*. Used cotton handkerchiefs filled with snot and blood, crumpled up on glass plates with sponge cake crumbs on the rims, screams from long gone souls, hidden for ever and ever in dark and eternally locked basements.

Happy children, dead children, children of all kinds. Faster and faster the pictures rushed through me. Pictures of bodies being dismembered as entertainment for television, pictures of newsreaders vomiting on prime time, filling all living rooms with cauterizing acids. Talk shows with hosts chanting their crazy jokes on and on forever, chasing a point which was just confirming the insanity against which it was supposed to anaesthetize all viewers. Intellectual, crazy and eternal thought combinations, sweating and copulating bodies puffing from unreleased lust, self-appointed seers and philosophers with egg heads as big as bombs, war and destruction, torn off limbs flying through the air, strapped-down drug addicts and molested children, obsequious world-saviours, self-glorifying gurus and devout, self-righteous holy men and women, row after row of carved-out people, manacled to fruit machines in gaming halls as big as hangars turning into endless rows of scarecrows on their way to mass graves at enormous stadiums where rock idols were turning and twisting in ecstatic auto-erotic spasms in front of a fascinated, drugged audience, a sea of people supervised by well-fed soldier-pigs in mud-brown uniforms. A hell as brown as hell itself. My own pain, my own repressions, judgements, prejudices, vanity, pornographic pictures, insane perversities, projections, an enormous choir of demons, the cries of witches and fornication, the truth about the human race – I could suddenly see – was the truth about myself!

The speed was now so high that I didn't have the strength to hold on. I let go with my fingertips and just had time to register the room I was in: the bed, the wallpaper, the table and the heater, before swirling away with the pictures which were changing at such speed and intensity that I knew that I was going insane. The pictures of hell were now mixed with pictures of radiating crosses, burning hearts and golden angel-like beings, grand scenarios of skies opening up, and I saw a being on a throne surrounded by an enormous halo glowing so strongly that it blinded me. The being was surrounded by cherubim and seraphim approaching me, and I saw that it was Christ piercing me at an enormous speed. But just when I was about to give in to this blessing, the being opened its mouth in a devilish grimace turning the flow of pictures inside out, deeper and deeper, higher and higher – until the tension became so strong that I screamed and screamed into the eternal darkness. But my screams drowned in the infernal noise, and I closed my eyes in order to avoid seeing the glowing horn – an enormous, erect penis on the forehead of the smiling Christ. And I saw that the penis was identical with the shaft through my solar plexus, that the pictures were my semen and that it was sterile.

Then the pictures stopped and the noise went silent. I was in a long subterranean passage. There was a pleasant temperature. Totally quiet. I walked through the passage towards a door that I knew I was going to open.

'*This is the lowest point – lower than Hades!*' the Voice said.

There was an indescribable calm, but also something fatal, something waiting to be seen. To be found out. Recognized.

I opened the door.

On a metal table in the middle of a room with a low ceiling, looking somewhat like an operating theatre with bare concrete walls, was an enormous cadaver, and I could see that it was a pig in a coma-like state. The pig's head was intact and carried a white, newly starched stand-up collar around its neck. Most of the meat was gone from the body, and behind the curved ribs I saw a big, bluish, beating heart, which was connected to an apparatus with a plastic hose, barely keeping the ill-fated creature alive.

'*Now you have seen it,*' the Voice stated.

And I floated through the room, in and out of doors, and suddenly I was in an enormous changing room where men and women with naked genitals sat on benches separated by clothes racks, reaching for each other without being able to make it while masturbating incessantly like crazy. Row upon row of pent-up souls, obsessed with lust. Lust for things, lust for fame, lust for attention, lust for money, lust for sex. And I saw how the desire and the obsession held these souls slave-bound in such a terrible limitation that I had to fight in order not to give in to the all-consuming fear. It wasn't just a row of identity-lacking individuals whom I was moving among – they were my brothers and sisters. I tried talking to some of them but they neither saw nor heard me. And I understood that I was just a guest and could move about freely, but also that I myself was once a prisoner here blinded by the chase for self-satisfaction. But I saw the longing behind the fear and the desires, the longing to be recognized, the longing for acceptance, the longing for love, the longing for freedom.

'*Now you have seen it!*' the Voice stated.

I was then lifted up through the shaft, back to the bed at the Hôtel Costes in Montségur, where I lay bathed in sweat and with every fibre of my body in burning pain from the cramp-like tightening of the muscles, and slowly it dawned on me that the nightmare was over. I was tired like someone who hadn't slept for a thousand years. I was, however, filled with a deep peace. I looked at my watch. It was five o'clock. I could just catch a few hours' sleep before getting back to the house. On waking up I knew immediately that something decisive had happened. My energies almost sparkled inside me. Getting out of bed a little later I felt light as a feather. And I understood that I had been through a cleansing during the night and had been liberated from burdens I had carried with me all through my life, well, maybe even since the beginning of time. It was quite clear that these burdens were basically something I had laid upon myself, that the pictures were shadows I had projected on to the world where they had changed into demons, the single purpose of which was to limit me in the most intricate ways and to stop me from doing what I came here to do. I was suddenly able to see how fleeting and illusory all these projections and pictures really are. How we let ourselves become tyrannized by our own basest beings, when, instead of changing the shadows, we create pictures of enemies and obstructions, which in turn create separation, distance, fear and war. Although feeling liberated at a deep level, there was still something I needed to recognize. The mere thought of the Christ-like figure made me shiver. And what was the difference between the radiating, angel-like Christ and the diabolical one with the erect penis-horn on his forehead?

'None! Both pictures are simply an expression of your own limited imaginings and projections,' the Voice answered. 'Christ can never be in opposition to himself. Christ is consciousness. Christ is One!'

Something very old moved deep inside me. The fear of sin. The fear of an angry and avenging and patriarch-like God. All that I thought I had let go of long ago opened like a pit of fear in my stomach. But contrary to my expectations it wasn't followed by one single picture. The fear was empty so to speak. A last desperate reaction from an old ailment?

Suddenly a warm laughter rolled through me – I do not know why. It was so unusual and took me by surprise to such a degree that I gave in to the liberating feeling of it without any kind of resistance. And suddenly it struck me that this was what the story about the expulsion from the temple was all about in the New Testament. The nocturnal cleansing was a kind of expulsion of my own inner Pharisees, moneylenders and merchants. It was a destruction of all the hypocritical masks, opinions, dubious visions and so-called 'good intentions' – my selfish care for others – with which I had betrayed and limited myself. All my sentimental and emotional imaginations about hate and love, good and evil, damnation and salvation, demons and angels, Christ and antichrist. All my conditions, my firm resistance. I was embarrassed just thinking about it. Not only because I had misled myself by hiding behind a one-sided front producing nothing but self-righteousness, but I was also embarrassed how arrogantly and stubbornly I had maintained the self-betrayal. Perhaps I was beginning to understand something about the thesis of my inner seer, that darkness is a series of hidden qualities which ought neither to be repressed nor demonized, but should be enlightened and transformed. And such a process demands a spiritual soberness. As the Seer used to say, you do not lend your car to a person who is very drunk – do you?

It was still dark as I started walking back to the house. As soon as I opened the door I was met by the smell of freshly made coffee. The Seer was packing a tent into a small canvas bag.

'Did you sleep well?'

It was not a question, more a statement of a fact that he knew. He simply saw how it radiated from me.

'So, so,' I said.

'There is coffee in the pot in the kitchen.'

I went to make breakfast. When a little later I sat watching him packing, I heard the Voice whispering:

'Only the one who is able to see his own face without a mirror is able to see his true character.'

Focusing, I tried to keep all other sounds away. This was important:

'*Looking without a mirror is not looking at objects, it is looking at THAT which is looking!*'

The tent moaned as the Seer tightened a knot.

'*A picture of God is not God. The word love is not love. You are not a Christian by saying so.*'

He formed a loop, pulled the string through it and tightened it with a quick pull. The Voice continued:

'*It is a matter of knowing that we are something else and more than a few ephemeral emotions in a transient body and the dubious personality we think we are.*'

He looked up and was surprised to see that I was watching him. Something had come between us. I went upstairs in order to pack my backpack. Half an hour later we were ready.

The contours of Montségur appeared like a picture revealed in a developing tray, silently, imperceptibly, without visible transitions. Prat was waiting for us, and when the Seer had talked to her he asked me to do the same.

I placed myself in front of the opening. Free of any expectation or idea about what I ought or should do. For a long time I just stood looking into the square without seeing anything.

'*Let go,*' the Voice whispered. '*Let go!*'

A certainty grew in my chest as imperceptibly as the dawn, a being with a consciousness as frail and intangible as ether and light. This was not a magnificent sight. Not a great vision. More of a silent fusing with silence. Here were no bicycles without brakes going down steep hills, no burning fires with tormented souls, no bathtubs with the water running out of them. No messages. Simply being. If I had had the courage I would have stepped into the square without hesitation. But intuitively I realized that this opening would always be available. That we, any time we so wish and any time we are

41

able to let go of all superfluous weight, have the possibility of stepping into this quiet freedom. My moment wasn't here yet. No one can stand in this square in a state of separation. You either do it totally or not at all. I opened my eyes. The Seer was smiling broadly.

We passed the steep, straight part of the mountain without any trouble. At the stile we turned right and found the path in the wilderness on the other side of the fence. I followed closely after the Seer. The path soon became both narrower and steeper. At many places it had totally disappeared and we had to keep our balance on fallen rocks or crossing the open mouth of the chasm. After an hour of difficult walking on the dramatic incline of the mountainside, the growth grew sparse. We stopped at a cliff shelf and had a wide view of the valley and the village below us. To the other side the Pyrenees stretched their snow-clad peaks towards the blue sky. We sat down on a large rock. The Seer's eyes met mine. I sensed that he was struggling with something that he couldn't handle. As he started to talk I saw him for the first time in his new role. Another, a more human side was appearing.

'There is something I must tell you. It is about time. And space. Although I have never been able to say who my employer is, you know that I have never doubted that it is the Board of Directors upstairs who are deciding the agenda.' He pointed towards the sky.

'I have never been able to understand all the talk about no man being able to stand the sight of God. For who and what is God? It's a question we must ask ourselves. All that about God is nonsense. God is an illusion. I think I have found a form of energy outside all the universes, the consciousness, if you like, which is the destiny of all things. Everything is predestined.'

His words felt like a frontal attack on the cosmic logic as I saw it. What was the meaning of everything if it was preordained? One could ask the question, who invented whom? Can God be defined by a name at all? In a religious context one might rightfully say that God is a relative conception, since that energy does not necessarily have the same value for everyone. Of course you may make the point that God is an illusion. That probably is the way it is whenever you try to limit that energy by putting a name to it. The name in itself does not say anything about the quality we normally call God. Might one even say that we have the kind of God that we have the imagination to imagine? Or that we have the kind of God we are able to perceive? But this only says something about us not about God.

He remained standing, looking up at the sky. An eagle circled overhead. Even though I felt his words in the physical realm, I couldn't help wondering whether there was something I earlier hadn't understood since he continued to belabour the point. The thought was barely formed before he smiled obligingly:

'You are right. I may be going too far.'

But I could hear in his voice that there was something else, something deeper. Something that maybe he himself didn't even know the meaning of.

'Blessed by Prat, we are now on our way to a dimension that I know nothing about. Get ready to register everything you see. That is why you are here. This is your task on this journey.'

'Where are we going?' I asked.

'Possibly into a series of events which have never been described before. If I knew, then we wouldn't have to go on.'

He got up and made me understand that we should start walking. I looked about for the eagle but it had disappeared. Suddenly it grew cold. The sun had disappeared behind a dark cloud. In front of me the Seer balanced elegantly at the edge of the cliff like a dancer. The path seemed to vanish into thin air. Below us the world disappeared. A strange rush into an unknown reality. Where was the focus? Were we walking on clouds? What was up and what was down? We crawled along the side of the mountain. Big beetle-like insects ran in and out between the rocks. With the tips of our fingers and the toes of our boots we inched around the cliff edge. All shapes disappeared into themselves. My thoughts flowed through me like a river which has surrendered and therefore must follow its own destiny. The path again became passable. But the sense of grounding was gone. Instead, a sparkling filigree of vibrating crystals appeared. The air was full of a radiant activity. It seemed as if someone had turned the switch on the ethereal membrane. I followed closely after the Seer who went through unimpeded. I felt a faint resistance, which made me stop for a brief moment. We penetrated the ethereal veil. At that moment the knot in my stomach was transformed into a sparrow, which was lifted, freed from its age-old burden into an unconditional kind of freedom. In front of me the Seer seemed to float. For a moment I fought to keep back my tears. Then I gave up and let them flow.

A cold, moist, scaly being touched my hand. I wanted to move my hand but couldn't let go of my last hold on earthly reality. Out of the corner of my eye I saw something move. Before turning my gaze in their direction I registered the presence of two intertwined snakes swaying in an inexplicable dance, brushing my hand. Surprisingly, this realization caused no panic in me. I simply registered it – probably because at a deeper level I was aware that what happened was unavoidable.

Ten metres in front of us and about three to four metres above us, a radiating square opened up. The Seer looked with rapt attention into it, but it didn't seem as if he recognized the figure in it. However, I had no doubt that it was a woman. The light around the figure grew stronger and I was almost lifted into the warm glow. The figure had a glowing radiance about her and I sensed that she was tall, well-proportioned and exceptionally beautiful. She wore her hair down her back and carried a wreath of small glittering lights around her head. For some reason I started to count them. There were twelve of them. I now noticed that the woman seemed to say something. I heard no words spoken and did not see her lips move. I just stared into this radiating being and felt a deep, deep sense of gratitude. Could this be the Virgin Mary? I tried to get closer to this being. But just as I asked the question, 'Who are you?' the Voice answered, 'The Bride.'

〰〰〰〰〰〰〰〰〰〰〰〰〰〰〰〰〰〰〰〰〰〰〰〰〰〰
〰〰〰〰〰〰〰〰〰〰〰〰〰〰〰〰〰〰〰〰〰〰〰〰〰〰
〰〰〰〰〰〰〰〰〰〰〰〰〰〰〰〰〰〰〰〰〰〰〰〰〰〰

The note came in waves from the sparkling filigree. A cosmic energy encircled the mountain like a vibrating tiara. Suddenly a section of the tiara moved forward and pulsated in front of me:

It lasted for a moment only, then the vibrations faded away. Frightened, I withdrew my hand at the same moment. The snakes disappeared from the rocks in the same movement. The Seer stood further ahead on the path seemingly lost in thought. The sun had disappeared and the clouds covered the sky. The cry of a bird echoed from the side of the cliff and reverberated through the valley, then disappeared into the growing mist.

We started walking. My sense of time was totally erased. Everything happened in a gliding movement. It struck me that although I felt like a spectator to a series of spectacular events, which were the result of the presence of an inexplicable force, I was still right in the middle of it. And although I was shaken to the core, on the other hand it didn't bother me at all. Everything happened so fast, or rather so much in a flow, that I didn't have the time to muster my usual reservations. It had never been a problem for me to accept the fact that forces existed which could not be experienced through our normal senses. However, I had never imagined that this was something in which I could actually participate. To be in the presence of the Power turned everything upside down. And I was beginning to realize that this Power first and foremost meant to break down any kind of reservation in me. What this energy really wanted was for me to step out from the trivial apathy of sleep, letting go of all my insane attempts to be 'right' or 'special', letting go of the fear of being alone and taking responsibility for the job in hand. Nevertheless, I was, at the same time, contemplating how I might communicate all these experiences in a credible way so that they were seen as realistic options rather than targets of ridicule, blown out of proportion and seen as the results of occult fantasy.

In just twenty-four hours I had experienced that there are more ways than one in which to see. I had experienced how shockingly easy it is to be led astray by the imagery created by our own minds and the large collective file of images in the lower astral regions, created by our repeated kow-towing, time and again, to limiting dogma and rigid interpretations. That they did not only consist of images of enemies but just as much of religious archetypes and symbols like Christianity's 'Yeshua on the cross', Buddhism's 'Buddha in the lotus position', as well as the long series of stereotypes used by the New Age movement. Not that there is anything wrong with these matrixes. They are inevitable and necessary in many connections, such as in education. Perhaps the Power simply wanted to show that the application of these images is of limited value when we are at the threshold of greater realizations. That only those with the courage to pass through the vale of shadows, enter the vale of soul-searching, cleanse themselves of all fixed notions and preconceptions and move beyond all limited ideas and symbols will gain admittance to these transcendent worlds and to this clarity of vision.

Imagine if all our age-old knowledge and symbolism, the images from the great collective unconscious, the Akasha archives in the ethereal worlds, all the great complex of cosmic language, no longer served their original purpose. Imagine, that they have become so worn and devalued because they are used and misused at every opportunity, that they have become our greatest limitation. The thought was almost unbearable. If this was the case, the whole foundation of religion and the humanities would collapse. How could humanity even get close to freedom without them?

I gave up on the thought and plodded along after the Seer.

He stopped at an overhang and placed his backpack on a rock overgrown with moss:

'We'd better have some lunch.'

As we were dividing the bread between us I wanted to ask him about the woman I had just seen.

He slowly chewed on a piece of baguette and looked at me in his usual subtle and surprised way.

'You haven't fallen in love – have you?'

He didn't wait for an answer:

'If I'm not wrong you must have seen an extraordinarily beautiful woman. Isn't that true?'

47

I nodded my assent. He smiled.

'I thought so. Let me put it this way, she apparently hasn't made herself known yet. But you must be patient. You have found a clue. We have been shown the right direction. We are surrounded by helpers, but it is important that we do not behave like two bulls in this unbelievably beautiful china shop.'

His look took on the intense focus that I knew so well. And now I saw what was happening, saw that he was about to make room so that I could come to my own realizations.

'*If man could see through his own blockages he would be able to understand how we all, quite uniquely and totally, are dependent upon cosmic laws whether we want it or not. But such an understanding must find its balance between intellect and heart in order to make a difference. All physical forms are made from molecules, but are, like all creatures and all things, concentrated, and, in most cases, still unchanged heavy energy. At the centre of this heaviness the qualities of light are hidden waiting to be activated. Man is also in constant movement, undergoing eternal change. Man is not only a being of particles but more than that he is a being of waves and vibrations. The field of energy you have just experienced you might call a door between the reality of particles and the reality of waves, a door to a more concentrated form of energy. Deep inside of you there was something recognizing this energy. And the only way for you to relate to this was to translate it into a recognizable image from the collective file. This image then showed itself on the ethereal membrane. That's the way it is and quite natural too. But it may soon turn into a limitation if you are not able to define the energy in the image, but instead let your interpretation of the quality of the energy become limited by the quality of the image itself. The God-energy is consciousness. Consciousness free from images. Consciousness as pure being.*'

(Painting by Peter Fich)

A warm feeling was spreading through my body and I expressed a quiet thank-you for the lecture. But another question needed an answer: who was this woman? And I heard myself asking the question of the inner Voice:

'Who was it that you saw?'

I didn't know who this *'you'* was at the time. And this ignorance was in itself precisely the most important witness to my insignificance and to the fact that I wasn't ready yet. For some seconds, which felt like light years, my question hovered, tensely. Finally the Voice answered:

'I saw the sea of light where this unique energy had its origin. I heard the poetry and the divine story in the sound from this sea. For a moment I disappeared in it – and I reappeared in the sea. And the sea is that woman, who is without a name, but whose daughters off and on appear in the world in order to restore the great vision and the correct sight. I came to this world from her womb. I was a suckling at her breast. I have drunk cosmic love from her mouth. I have seen everything in her eyes. I was given the sign on her forehead and at the sight of the twelve stars in her hair – I remember the certainty within which I have my origin.'

Moved, I gazed at the mountain whilst these gripping words sang through the stillness. Who was it that spoke? What was the sign that the Voice was talking about? The same kind of warm glow that I had seen around the woman now also radiated from the words. It was so simple and so beautiful that all my writings here – now – are nothing but withered flowers.

The Seer looked at me with an intense sadness, as if the sight of me could help recall a long-gone feeling of happiness, which was no longer his. He smiled. Then he said:

'You had a question?'

'Well, when I saw her I thought that she might be the

Virgin Mary. But when I asked about it, a voice said that she was the Bride. What do you think?'

'I think that this feminine energy is quite different from the well-known one: the mother, *mater*, the feminine which has always been identified with yielding, being receptive, giving birth, the moist, the dark, the nurturing, passive and negative principle in nature. I'm in no doubt that what you have received here is quite another and much stronger, more embracing and superior form of energy. I cannot say any more at the moment. Just that we are on the right track. It is not every day that one gets to see something like that.'

He laughed aloud at the last remark and stretched out in the moss like a knight who has just remembered the princess, partly feeling sad and partly yearning for her.

We camped at the old stronghold area of the Cathars in a small forest a few hundred metres from the top of the mountain. I started unpacking the tent while the Seer found an abandoned eagle's nest where he spent the rest of the day.

I found a reasonably level place suitable for setting up the tent in the middle of the paved area, where the stronghold must have been. There was a touching seriousness and quietness here and I made myself believe that I could feel the presence of the *perfecti*, who died in the struggle with the soldiers of the Inquisition during the month of February 1244. The stronghold had been the most important defence of the Cathars, and when that fell the enemy used the ledge to set up the feared catapults, the trébuchets. That was the beginning of the end for the Cathars. They surrendered on 7 March 1244 and were given the choice of either renouncing their faith and converting to the Church of Rome or being burnt at the stake. All chose the stake except the three *perfecti* who were sent off with the secret treasure of the Cathars under cover of darkness.

It was dark when the Seer returned to the tent. He seemed to be more serene than he had been earlier in the day. I had collected brushwood for a small fire. Supper consisted of bread and water. We sat in silence for a long time watching the stars in the sky. The Cathars and their treasure had occupied my thoughts most of the day just as they had done for many other people before me. I broke the silence:

'What do you know about the treasure that the Cathars are supposed to have had and which was removed from the fortress shortly before they surrendered?'

'Just a moment,' he answered and disappeared into his usual trance-like state. However, he soon came back:

'So many legends are connected to this treasure. It is said that the Grail may be a possibility. No one has considered the possibility that it might have something to do with a kind of knowledge that should definitely not get lost; knowledge that might have been put in writing or hidden in the memories of three Cathars, which had to be transported away from Montségur in order not to fall into the hands of the Church of Rome or to disappear forever.'

'What kind of knowledge?'

'Well, that is a very good question. This, among other things, is one of the reasons why we are here. And the experiences that you have had may play an important part here.'

His familiar look underlined that what he was about to say was of the utmost importance:

'If you really want to put a name to the woman we met, then I know that you can do it. All you have to do is ask *out there*.'

He let the sentence hang in the air. But it didn't hang there for long before the name of the mystical woman manifested itself as though it was the most natural thing in the world to do so.

'Mariam Magdal!'

We sat in the quiet of the moment. The Seer then broke it:

'Who is she?' he asked and looked questioningly at me.

I couldn't help smiling. I had totally forgotten that the Seer wasn't in the least interested in the dogma of the Christian church and that his understanding of Christianity was solely based upon what he was able to see – and not what was to be found in its writings. This, however, meant that someone had to ask him the relevant question.

'Mariam Magdal is Aramaic for Mary Magdalene,' I answered. 'Mariam may mean "*the joy of God*", "*the spirit of Peace*" or in certain dialects "*princess*", whereas Magdal means '*She of the watchtower*'. In Malachi's book from the Old Testament the expression *Magdal-eder* is known, which means something like "*The Exalted One*", "*the Protector of the Flock*" or "*the One Who is elevated and is guarding the others*" or a mixture of these. A kind of royal figure who is a leader and a protective light for her subjects. All in all, the name Mary Magdalene could mean "*The Spirit of the Exalted Peace*".'

He nodded with an air of being interested:

'And what does the professor know about her?'

'The New Testament does not say much about her. She is mentioned by name perhaps only a dozen times and there is a theory that Mariam, that is Mary Magdalene, and Mary of Bethany are one and the same.

'If this is the case then she is the sister of Martha, Mari and Lazarus whom, according to the gospels, Yeshua raised from the dead. She was present at the crucifixion and according to John's Gospel was the first to see the risen Yeshua at the tomb. In the Gospel of Luke there are references to a 'sinner', a woman who is supposed to have been a prostitute. During his visit to Simon the Pharisee's house, this woman washes Yeshua's feet anointing them with ointment. The woman washed Yeshua's feet with her tears and wiped them with her hair, kissed his feet and anointed them with ointment from an alabaster jar. Simon the Pharisee clearly indicates by his attitude to her that she is "untouchable".

'The identification of the "sinner" in Luke's Gospel as a prostitute was determined by Pope Gregory in the year 591. He declared that the unnamed woman in this gospel was indeed Mary Magdalene, the woman "out of whom went seven devils" and he announced that all true believers should regard her as the prostitute who was converted and saved after Yeshua exorcised her of seven evil spirits. If you look at the Greek word for prostitute that Pope Gregory used to describe Mariam – *harmatolos* – it can be translated in various ways. From a Jewish perspective it can mean someone who has broken the law. It may also mean someone who has not paid their taxes. The Greek word *porin*, woman of easy virtue, which is used in other parts of Luke, is not the word used for the "sinner" who washes Yeshua's feet with her tears and dries them with her hair. Thus nowhere in the New Testament does it state that Mary Magdalene was a prostitute.'

I stopped in order to see if he was bored.

'Do go on,' he said, 'it is very interesting.'

'In St Mark's Gospel, we read of the second time Mariam anoints Yeshua who remarks "Verily I say, wherever this gospel is preached throughout the world, what she has done will also be spoken of in memory of her." Unfortunately, it seems that this has not been done in very many Christian congregations.

'We are also told that Yeshua exorcised seven devils or evil spirits from her. Pope Gregory felt that they were the seven deadly sins.'

I stopped again to be quite sure that he really wanted to hear more. But he impatiently motioned me to continue.

'So much for the Church and its writings. If we take a look at some of the Gnostic and apocryphal writings, the Nag Hammadi scrolls and *Pistis Sophia*, which might have been among those that Constantine the Great and the bishops decided were heretical in the year 325, there unfolds a totally different story. It was on this same occasion that they decided that "the right faith" should be based on the scriptures, which we know today as the New Testament. Furthermore, they took steps to make the corrections in the texts which present-day research has finally considered to be just that, corrections. All other non-Christian sources were banned by the synod. It looks, therefore, as if much of the Christian teachings in the churches today are, in many areas, far removed from those of Yeshua two thousand years ago. Quite a thought – eh?'

The Seer nodded and threw more brushwood on the fire.

'What do the heretical writings say about our Mariam?'

'We are told in *The Gospel of Mary* that she was blest with visions and a deeper understanding than Peter. She is the one who teaches and comforts the other disciples. In *The Dialogue with the Saviour* she is praised not only as a psychic but also as the apostle surpassing all the others. She was "the woman who knew the universe". In *The Gospel of Phillip* it is said that she was the companion of Yeshua:

"The companion of the Saviour is Mary Magdalene. He loved her more than all the disciples and often kissed her on the mouth.

"There were three who always walked with the lord: his mother, Mary, his sister and Magdalene, the one who was called his companion. His sister and his mother and his companion were each called Mariam."

'Yeshua says in *Pistis Sophia*:

"Where I am my twelve disciples shall be, but Mariam

Magdalene and Yohannan, the Virgin, are above all my disciples and above all people who are to receive the unspeakable mystery. And they shall be to my right and to my left. And I am they and they are me.

"Mariam, thou blessed one, whom I shall teach the highest mysteries, speak, since you are the one whose heart is closer to Heaven than all your brothers.'"

The Seer was listening with his eyes closed. When I went silent he opened them and looked enquiringly at me:

'Is that all?'

I searched my brain but couldn't think of anything else.

We sat for a while. The Seer got up and stretched his arms above his head:

'I'm quite certain that we have taken a considerable step forward in our quest. We'd better get some sleep.'

He put his sleeping bag under his arm and pointed to the tent:

'The tent is for you. I'll sleep in my little eagle's nest. Sweet dreams.'

I looked at him as he walked along the slope until he was just a shadow between the trees. Then he disappeared in the dark. The stars twinkled in the sky.

I sat for a while before going to bed. But I couldn't sleep. For some reason the thought persisted that there was something I had forgotten, something which might answer the Seer's question more precisely.

I do not know how long I kept tossing and turning unable to rest. Then suddenly it struck me. The answer. The only book I had brought with me was *The Gospel of The Holy Twelve*. As usual, not recognized by orthodox scholars, this work was received in a vision and translated from Aramaic in 1900 by a clairvoyant English minister, G J Ouseley. I simply love it for its highly poetic language and its purity of the first water

56

(pure weight in gold!). I quickly got up and fished the book out of my backpack and leafed through it until the torchlight swept across a page at random.

Chapter 66, verse 7: Thus it is with the One, the Father-Mother, in whom is neither male nor female and in whom are both, and each is threefold and all are One in the hidden Unity.

Verse 8: Marvel not at this, for as it is above so it is below, and as it is below so it is above, and that which is on earth is so, because it is so in Heaven.

Verse 9: Again I say unto you, I and My Bride are one, even as Maria Magdalena, whom I have chosen and sanctified unto Myself as an example, is one with Me.

'I and My Bride are one,' and 'Maria Magdalena, whom I have chosen as an example'. These statements expressed their own unmistakable language. The rest might have been taken directly from the *Gospel of Thomas*. There was just one small objection: *The Gospel of The Holy Twelve* was translated and published 55 years before the *Gospel of Thomas* emerged from the sands of Egypt.

I turned off the lamp and put the book aside.

'Maria Magdalena, whom I have chosen as an example.'

'I and My Bride are one.'

Then I fell asleep.

4

Lazarus looked like a ghost in the pale morning light. She embraced him while the camels were made ready for the journey.

'In Beersheba you'll find Isaac the Pious One at the town square. One of Those Dressed in White will be waiting for you. He will bring you safely through the desert to Heliopolis.'

His nervousness broke out with full force as he started hurrying the guards who were busy stowing the luggage. It was important to get started before the sun rose. It was in the middle of Tammuz and they were about to cross the Judea Desert.

'What must happen will happen,' she said smilingly.

As the small caravan silently passed the gate she turned around once and waved at her brother and two sisters. She was already on her way into another world. Out of the reality of blood and into the reality of spirit.

They travelled through Bethlehem unnoticed. The roads were full of Roman patrols. Around noon she sat drowsily on her camel watching the three guards and her maid who flickered like a mirage in the scorching sun. The unnerving sound of the monotonous thump of saddlebags against the flank of the camel was interrupted only by the whining of the maid. Mariam herself sat silently in her saddle.

They rode up into the hills surrounding Hebron in order to pass the town unseen, the town where Abraham's wife, Sara, was buried and where King David at one time was anointed king of the House of Judea. Coming out of the valleys they rode into a rough wind that lifted the sand, throwing it into the air in burning clouds that pricked the skin of the travellers like needles. One of the guards looked at her questioningly, seeking for the long-awaited sign to stop and rest. But she didn't say anything, pretending that she hadn't seen. Instead, she lost herself in the swaying rhythm of the camel's hips, fusing with its lazy movements beneath her as she slipped into a meditative state.

They reached the Town of the Seven Wells, Beersheba, in the late afternoon without having stopped once. Isaac the Pious One helped her off the camel himself. The guards tried to look as if they had kept their composure while the maid had to be carried into the travellers' quarters.

'You look as if you could do with a bath,' Isaac said.

Drops of sweat had made thin, marbled patterns in the mask of sand grains on Mariam's face. But she just smiled as if she knew that the wildness of her beauty was simply enhanced by signs of the rigours of travelling.

This was her first experience of the hospitality of the Brotherhood. She washed herself in the pool behind a small pillared hall and was quietly amused by the curious eyes staring at her from the shadows, as if she were a strange being from an unknown world. Even holy eyes have to rest on the beauty of transience she thought while she generously took her time.

Isaac blessed their evening meal and prayed the necessary prayers. They dined in silence. Afterwards he took her up to the roof of the house where they had a view of the town. He pointed towards the desert:

'Out there is the Negev, the anvil of the sun. You are young and may not know the significance of the journey you have set out on. You are beautiful, more beautiful than anyone else. But I do not see in you the deceit that is nurtured by vanity. Tread softly, Mariam, for men will seek intimacy with you. Do not let yourself be tempted and do not tempt anyone. Out there is the Negev. Behind its apparent beauty and luxuriance it hides its true character. We call it the Oven of Souls, the Desert of Purification and Transformation. No one travels through it and remains the same. But I see that you possess great courage. Do you also have the strength, I wonder?'

He became silent and she sensed how his words disappeared in the dusk. Their simple power spread through her and a quiet calm rose up from her stomach.

'Tomorrow, one of the brothers will accompany you through the desert and on to your goal. You and I shall not see each other again. Be aware of my words and guard your virtue. May the Holy Spirit be with you.'

He turned around and disappeared in the darkness without having looked at her once. His words and whole demeanour were devoid of any sentimentality. But she still sensed his warm feelings, like the feelings of a father embracing his daughter. Yet behind all of that she glimpsed something fate-laden, a dark shadow moving across the already cloudy sky. She fell asleep with this shadow watching over her.

She woke up early. The sky was grey and there was a nip in the air; it was cool. The shadow had gone, but the feeling of oppression from the previous evening still seized her. She washed herself, packed her few belongings and walked out into the grey morning without having any of the food that the brothers had set out for her and her two guards. There was no sign of the maid and she thought that it was better that the maid stayed where she was safe. The brothers were performing their service at the Holy of Holies in the synagogue.

She was watching the camels being prepared when suddenly she noticed a tall lean figure wearing a cloak and sitting on a mule by the gate at the outskirts of the yard. The figure had an almost radiating and unreal aura about it as if it floated in the air. The image disturbed her without her immediately knowing why. Not until the camels had been loaded up and the guards had led them out into the open did she realize that the figure was the brother who was going to lead them through the desert to Heliopolis. The thought restored her courage.

The small caravan moved out in the silence of the morning. The cloaked one was leading the caravan up ahead. Mariam nudged the camel to make it move faster in order to get to the stranger, but inexplicably the mule of the cloaked one seemed to hover along over the red-brown sand as if it had no connection with the ground. No matter how fast she rode the figure kept his distance about 20 metres ahead of her.

Except for a short break in the middle of the day, where they found shelter below an overhang while the sun passed the anvil, they kept on riding until darkness enveloped them.

When they rode through the gate of El Akish, the biggest caravanserai on the road, she felt the toil of the day in all her limbs. She couldn't see anything but sensed that the sea was not far away, and she thought that old Isaac had exaggerated in his talk about the oven of the soul.

In silence they rode through the narrow alleys until they stopped in a courtyard outside a house on the outskirts of the caravanserai. In the dark she noticed various figures taking care of the animals and searched for the cloaked one, but a bonfire in the yard made shapes flicker in the cracks of the walls and she lost her orientation.

A woman's voice reached her in the dark. It sounded as if it came from the fire where more and more figures assembled. The voice became more and more insistent, without Mariam being able to hear what it was saying. There was something in it that drew her closer, something that made her forget her fatigue.

She found a place among the seated figures where she could hear the female storyteller, but she couldn't see her.

'There is only *Rukha d'koodsha* – the holy breath. There is only this vibration, coming from that breath, expanding through the universe and becoming a part of you. The song of the breath sings: "Oh, daughters of Zion. Where have you hidden your virtue? Where have you hidden your ability to love? Where have you hidden the bride, the bride waiting for the groom?" And the breath is singing: "Alas, the sons of Zion. Where have you hidden your humility? Where have you hidden your ability to give yourselves without wasting your semen? Where have you hidden the groom? The groom who is seeking his bride."'

The woman stopped in order to emphasize the words which held the listeners spellbound.

'The celestial Queen is rising from the age-old sea. Her power has fallen from the sky. She opens her heart for everything created. She is devoted to you. She offers herself to you but you – you are tearing her womb apart and sullying her purity. Listen you sons and daughters of Zion. I come to those whose heart has been broken on my behalf. I raise the one who has fallen and I heal anyone who comes to me. Open yourselves to my power. Receive the Holy One for your days on earth are running out – whereas eternal life is waiting for you in every word I speak.'

The voice stopped once more for effect. Mariam leaned forward in order to get a glimpse of the person who could speak like this.

'If you want to, I can lead you to the living water and the heavenly fire. But if you doubt me you will be left to yourselves. The one who wants to save himself must forfeit his life. The one who gives himself shall gain eternal life – transformed, exalted. Forever radiating in my heaven, which is without beginning and without end. Step forward you who doubt these words.'

Time stood still around the bonfire. No one moved. Everybody sat entranced.

Then the silence was broken. A man stood up and pointed accusingly at the woman, whom Mariam couldn't see but whose words had touched her so deeply. The man's words were heavily judgemental:

'How dare you talk to decent people like this, you presumptuous one, you altar of immorality?'

A shiver went through the gathering. The man now spoke directly to them:

'Do you not know that this woman is a whore, that she is Helen of Tyrus?'

The eyes of the man glinted in the light from the flames reaching towards the sky.

Mariam *saw* him. She saw his fear, his intense lechery filled with anger. She saw his longing and his lack of love.

The gathering moved restlessly. They didn't know what to believe. They had heard all the various rumours about Simon the Magician and his woman, the transformed whore Helen. They had heard many terrible but also many wonderful things. The rumour about this immoral woman had also reached their part of the country. But how were they to connect these rumours with the woman whose words had reached the hearts of all so directly, and which had made them spellbound. Words from another world, far away from dust and sweat and blood and saliva. Far from lechery, sacrifice, hate, revenge and devilish magic. Words which could come from Heaven alone.

'How dare you!' the man shouted and lifted his arm to throw the stone he had just picked up from the ground.

Suddenly the exalted mood from earlier changed to fear. Everybody jumped to their feet and spread out. Some bent over to pick up stones to throw. Mariam caught one of them by the arm but was punched by a fist and thrown to the ground.

'Get thee hence, woman,' shouted the man whose actions she had tried to stop.

The stones flew through the air but, lying on the ground, Mariam saw to her surprise that Helen, the target of the men's anger, had apparently disappeared into the darkness. In their confusion and frustration the men threw the stones in all directions, as if in this way they hoped to stop the sound of the voice whose echo was still hanging in the emptiness, reminding them of something they had forgotten and did not want to be reminded of. Mariam saw it all.

Then she was lifted into the air. She felt the coarse groping of hands and how they sought out the most intimate parts of her body, greedily and without shame. She tried to twist away from the stranger's grip, but then noticed that it was one of the guards holding her in his arms. She wanted to shout to him that he should put her down, but the words disappeared in the noise from the agitated throng of people. He carried her to a house behind a large building facing the yard.

There was an open fire in the house. Not until she was sitting in front of the fire did she regain her composure. One of Those Dressed in White was preparing a ritual of the Brotherhood and she deduced that she was in one of their secret haunts. Mariam looked about but the cloaked one was not to be seen. Then the words of the mysterious woman came to mind, and she felt how they filled her and penetrated her heart.

Who was this Helen? Where had she gone to?

Mariam came to when one of the brothers offered her the chalice with the Power of the Spirit. As a woman and as a guest in the house of the brothers it was her privilege to be the first one to receive this communion. The oldest of the brothers performed the prayer.

'And remember, woman, that it is your choice whether or not you want to receive the chalice or let it pass you by. Receive the Gift of the Eternal One. Go into his house. Or leave his path forever.'

She lifted the chalice with trembling hands. Her blood froze at the words of the older brother. The underlying note boded doom and eternal fire. She drank quickly and immediately passed it on. Did she have a choice?

Later she sat alone at the fire and got lost in the flames. One of the brothers came in and hesitatingly sat down beside her, as if sent to answer the questions burning on her lips.

'Who is this Helen?' she asked.

'You haven't heard about her?' the brother answered.

'Should I have?'

'Only because it is now publicly known. Sixty days ago it was still a secret and I wouldn't have been able to tell you. But now it is of course a quite different situation. And since you are not just anybody it doesn't matter if I tell you or you hear it from someone else.'

She looked surprised at the brother.

'What do you mean, "I'm not just anybody"?'

He looked at her just as surprised.

'We know your brother, Lazarus,' he answered haltingly, as if he had said too much after all.

'And?'

He looked at her more and more incredulously. He really couldn't understand that maybe she knew nothing.

'Tell me!' she said eagerly.

'Lazarus has been initiated into our Brotherhood. He is a novice in the Brotherhood and has been appointed to take care of an important task, about which I cannot tell you.'

She felt the disappointment spreading in her. She was only something special because of Lazarus' position in the Brotherhood. Not that she wasn't happy and proud of him, but as she heard the words of the One Dressed in White she had hoped to be recognized for who and what she was in her own right. But how could they know what she was able to see?

The One Dressed in White continued:

'A candidate from Samaria, Simon the Magician, brought the woman, Helen, here from Tyrus. He has jeopardized his candidature for the sake of this woman. Now she has become an itinerant preacher. This has caused a great uproar among the high priests in Jerusalem, not to mention among the brothers at Carmel and in Qumran. The Sanhedrin in

Jerusalem accuse the Brotherhood of deliberately wanting to cause indignation and separation among the people. And this though they know very well that Those who Dress in White always operate in secrecy. This Simon and his woman Helen operate autonomously. And it has gone so far that Simon can no longer control her madness. It is blasphemy of the Lord.'

Mariam felt her throat tighten. The words of the One Dressed in White made her uncomfortable. Then she said:

'Did you not hear the woman's speech at the bonfire?'

'Why should I listen to something like that voluntarily?'

'Because she may just be speaking the truth. Because she spoke the word of the Lord. I have never heard anyone talk like that. Did you not see how her words captured her listeners?'

The One Dressed in White got up:

'I saw how she agitated the people with her blasphemous talk. This is hardly the will of the Lord. They have made a snake's nest of magicians and false prophets out of His sanctuary. This kind of thing has always been able to spellbind the people. They say that she speaks in order to scandalize and create discord. That she is spreading the work of Satan to the ignorant ones.'

'It was only a matter of a few men. Men who . . .'

She went silent. The brother had turned his back on her. She saw that he didn't want to hear any more. Then she had a sudden thought:

'What do you know about Yeshua?'

The question stopped him in his tracks as he moved away from her. Mariam knew that the One Dressed in White knew. He turned towards her:

'Yeshua?'

'Yeshua ben Yoasaph,' she insisted in order to hold his attention.

Their eyes met for a moment but he quickly looked away.

'I – I do not know anyone by that name.'

He continued to move away from her. She let him go. Unwillingly, he had given her the answer she wanted.

She waited until everybody had gone to bed. Then she quietly slipped into the open. The air was fresh. A strange mingling of sea and desert. High in the sky a single star twinkled, imitating the star in her chest. In the dark she sensed a figure in the yard. She stood still for a moment like a doe sensing danger. She recognized the Cloaked One and wanted to call out to him. Then she moved towards him across the yard but he kept moving away so that the distance between them remained the same.

They walked through the sleeping town. She walked briskly but couldn't get any closer to him. She hardly noticed that they had left the town and were on their way into the desert.

She woke up quite disorientated and couldn't recognize the room she was in. She didn't get up but tried to find her bearings. Then she remembered the woman, Helen, and her burning speech. Strange how words could be so intense and enthral you so deeply. She sensed the desert of the previous night deep inside her but couldn't remember the details and therefore let it go. However, she was aware of just one thing, she had to find this Helen.

She got up and got dressed. Downstairs the brothers were already performing their first communion. One hour later she and her two guards were on their way again.

In front of them the Cloaked One was straddling his mule. Again it was as if both rider and animal were floating over the sand. Mariam made an effort to find the rhythm of her own animal but her back was stiff and she had fire in her hips. It was the time of the moon. Out of the corner of her eye she watched the guard who had taken her into the house the previous evening. He was an inveterate warrior, but of a special kind whose only purpose was attack and defence. He had a tough face with dark, leathery features. His body was muscular and sunburned. She wondered if he had a woman and a family waiting for him somewhere, or if, like most men of his kind, he had dedicated himself totally to the life of a warrior. She remembered his hands that so brutally groped her body, but strangely enough, this didn't make her angry. Instead, she felt that she understood the man and his needs. At a deeper level she understood that he wasn't evil, but was the result of a choice that others had made for him a long time ago. In him she saw the most basic needs of man expressed. An almost animal-like being of instinct, carried along by a strange, purposeful strength with human features, but who had totally repressed all forms of human dignity. She saw, in every fibre of his body, in his tough and precise movements, his sexual nature bound up with survival instinct and fear of death that trickled like beads of sweat over his muscles, which flexed and relaxed, flexed and relaxed, flexed and relaxed. She understood that no man can harbour such an urge and such fear of death and not constantly seek release from it. She understood why such men sought comfort and kindness from prostitutes. They didn't know anything else. She understood them because she *saw* them. But it made her sad and disheartened. She saw at the same time that it was this fear of death, which turned the world into a cesspool of darkness, where men struggled forward on tottering feet of clay. For unknown reasons this made her think of the man to whom she was betrothed, and waves of an old sorrow moved through her. Where was he now? Did he also dream about a woman, about family and children? And if he did, was she this woman? Her thoughts went round and round and, as so many times before, they made her feel more and more hopeless. This was indeed a relentless desert.

In the afternoon they passed a unit of Roman soldiers without being accosted, as if Mariam and the guards were invisible. Everything happened in a daze. The Cloaked One had suddenly disappeared. They camped in the evening, sheltered by cliffs and not far from the sea. The guards kept their distance. The fire in her abdomen was at its highest. The pain filled her totally, but she understood that it kept her in contact with the world and the earth on which she walked. Her only thought was her wish to see the charismatic Helen once more.

They got to the ferry across the Nile at Lape two days later.

'Blessed be you daughter of Isis,' the blind ferryboat woman called out to Mariam, as they reached the other bank where a totally new world waited for them. The change from barren desert, with rugged cliffs, to flat and fertile delta mirrored a similar change in her. Along the roads were strange sculptures of animal-like beings, gods from another world, ornamented with all kinds of sacrifices. Everywhere well-kept fields of grain and oases with fig and balm trees. As they passed them, the farmers greeted them with smiles and positive gestures. Even the light seemed milder in this country and she was filled with hope.

Heliopolis was a dream of white marble and bright sandstone with magnificent wide avenues and temples of all kinds. However, the whole town seemed to be built around one single building, the goal of Mariam's journey, the gigantic Temple of Isis in the centre of the town. It was in this temple that Moses used to be the high priest and it was from here that he had set out to take the Jews back to the Holy Land.

The renown of the Temple of Isis had spread as far as Rome. Of all holy places, this was praised as the most magnificent.

Mariam felt dizzy as slowly she ascended the wide staircase. The moment she entered the town she was overwhelmed by a mood of inexplicable resignation, which stunned her and cut her off from contact with the forces with which she was gradually becoming familiar. She now felt totally abandoned by everyone and everything and was only able to see the devilish beauty, the predictable and bombastic result of man's limited idea of the Holy Force, forever depicted in marble, sandstone and mortar.

She heard women's voices singing from afar and behind them a chanting male voice, everything in a language that she didn't understand. Unresistingly she surrendered into unknown hands – hands, which carefully held her and led her through magnificently decorated halls, wonderful gardens with fantastic sculptures and imaginative fountains. She hardly noticed that she was undressed, washed and given a strange new gown to wear. She did not resist as they held a cup with a bitter drink to her lips and gently but firmly forced her to drink it. After that she lost all sense of time.

The character of the journey changed. She was now surrounded by figures with animal heads acting in another world from the one she was in. Even the character of the sounds changed and she had to give up trying to understand the language that was spoken by these figures. She hovered in an indefinable void, fell into a dissolving sphere and changed into nothingness, which showed itself in the form of an opening through which the animals passed freely. In her few, clear moments she thought that she had gone mad or that she was dead and that this diabolical place was some sort of weird paradise or a very refined sort of hell. She understood that basically she was just a thought. It was a liberating acknowledgement and the freedom lifted the thought towards a warm light of a nobler lineage. Only one single question threatened to undermine her newly won liberty: Who was thinking this thought? To whom did it belong?

She opened her eyes and stared into a sky full of twinkling stars. She turned her head and realized that she was lying on a cot in a room with high walls and a large opening in the ceiling through which she could see the night sky. The room was devoid of furniture except for a chair on which a young girl was sitting.

The girl was watching Mariam. They were of the same age. Their eyes met and the girl smiled when she saw that Mariam was awake.

'How are you?' the girl asked.

Mariam tried to remember what had happened, but she was too confused to think clearly. Instead she asked:

'Where am I?'

'In the Temple to Isis in Heliopolis,' the girl answered.

'What happened? Why am I lying here?'

The girl got up and came closer to Mariam.

'You came a month ago. In the meantime you have been through the initial rituals.'

She was now standing by the cot and carefully placed her hand on Mariam's shoulder. Her touch made Mariam relax, and she thought that the girl must have magic hands.

'What rituals?'

'The rituals necessary to erase the memory of your former life.'

Mariam left the question for the time being and surrendered to the girl's hands, which were quietly massaging her shoulders.

'My name is Ani. My task is to take care of you. It looks as if they expect a lot from you. Even Atuka has mentioned you in his prayers.'

Mariam grew tense at the sound of this name. Her mind worked hard in order to remember, but everything went around in a circle and there was no opening. She then asked the most logical question:

'Who is Atuka?'

Ani looked at her with disbelief:

'Atuka is the high priest and the substitute for Osiris in this temple. He is the one who will be in charge of your initiation if ever you get that far. Be quiet now. You need your rest. Your education starts tomorrow.'

Mariam held on to the moment:

'How long have you been here?' she asked.

'I grew up here.'

Ani's hands moved in gentle circles, and Mariam gave up looking for more questions. Instead, she got lost in the multitude of stars on the ceiling. Something told her that the answer was somewhere up there.

5

I see seven beautiful women in long, transparent robes on a stage where, as an actor, I'm playing Hamlet's uncle. They stand in a circle intensely occupied by something. I cannot see the faces of the women very clearly, but I feel their sensual beauty. When I call to them they step aside, turn towards me with naked breasts and let go of whatever they are holding. It turns out to be a dim sphere of light hopping about like a ball with too little air in it. It jumps in my direction and rolls over and comes to a stop at my feet. I pick it up, look at it astonished, realizing that it is the planet Uranus. I then turn towards the audience, holding Uranus in front of me like Hamlet holding the skull and say, 'The King is dead – Long live the King!'

The sound and smell of burning brushwood reached me from outside, where the Seer was already sitting on his rock by the fire waiting for the water in the small pot to boil for the first cup of coffee of the day.

'So, did the professor sleep well?'

The new day felt like an embrace. There was an immediacy and naturalness, an easiness and a pure presence, liberating everything and transforming these minutes into a moment that would never pass. It was in situations like these that I felt I got a glimpse of that which is always present, but which is seldom appreciated because I'm doing something else. And without being able to explain it better, it was in this state I began getting in contact with my higher qualities. Perhaps because this sphere in all its simplicity was certainty itself.

A little later, when I was sitting opposite him, I told him about my dream. He looked into the fire for a long time before answering:

'The dream tells you that you must take your Uranus work upon you. The seven women may be the Pleiades, however, they may also mean the seven old planet worlds. Uranus like Pluto is one of the new ones. You must give new life to Uranus by moving the authorities – the world's and your own – but without you being tempted to become too self-centred. You must be able to put yourself outside of all conditions and all norms whatever they may be. You are present but not necessarily visible.'

He disappeared for a moment, but then came back:

'Remember, a smile spreads like rings in water. It starts a chain reaction and may create a revolution. Changing war into peace. It is not important who started the process. The important thing is to get it started. Give Caesar what belongs to Caesar. But no more than that. Remember, when you are waiting for the traffic lights to change from red into green – even if there are no cars – Caesar still breaks the law as much as he likes. And who says that the light will ever change into green? Isn't traffic regulated on Caesar's bidding? That is why you have to accept breaking the law of Caesar and cross on a red light when it is necessary. It is your responsibility. But be careful, so that you are not run over. The ninth planet, Pluto, is presented at the death of the little "I". Hamlet's uncle is that I. This is what you now renounce. You'll wake up with a hangover, in the King's bed, thinking that you are dreaming. But you are not. You have just wakened to the real world. You are now sober and may take on a responsibility – but you remain invisible. Pluto is also resurrection.'

He gazed vacantly into the distance. I had never experienced him like that before. After a while he looked focused again.

'Uranus is the planet of the wizard. In your dream it is the connection between you and Sirius.'

He closed his eyes:

'This is how you received the gift when you were about ten years old. The kundalini experiences you had then, which were caused by the shock over the death of your sister combined with your sexual awakening, were the result at a higher level of the flow from Sirius via Uranus and Venus to the kundalini centre in you. This opened your ability to see. But it was so powerful and overwhelming that you couldn't handle this gift, because at the moment of release it connected you with all the incarnations in which you were not able to release and use that power. And it is quite clear that such an experience brings a lot of pain with it. But now you must take the responsibility upon you, the responsibility which at the time accompanied this gift.'

'But how?'

'By staying awake and listening to what is being said. By *seeing*!'

The teasing smile became serious.

'You may trust the Board of Directors with the rest. Be sure that they will let you know when the time is at hand. First and foremost, it is important that you are aware of the correct situation and that you do not turn your back on this consciousness.'

I was contemplating his answer when suddenly I wanted to know how he had experienced *his* awakening.

'How did it happen for you?' I asked.

'Well, I also experienced great confusion. It can be quite a strain on your body because not all of the organs of the body are necessarily "open" and directed towards the poles corresponding to the flow of energy. And if you do not understand what is going on, well, then it can be quite chaotic. I was under great pressure. It was a symbol of the purification I had to go through on a higher level as well, a re-definition of the aspect of my will or the power, if you like. After that it went quite painlessly. A language was being born in me. A dictionary appeared along with that language, which gave me an immediate understanding. Suddenly I *knew*! There were no doubts. I began seeing connections far beyond the universe, well, even further out, far beyond all universes. Back to Creation – and even before that.'

'But how did you begin to integrate it?'

'I first had to go through the well-known children's diseases. You know, I thought I was a hell of guy – well, pardon my French – but that was what I was. The circumstances forced me to look at my motives. When I started working with my clients it all became self-regulating. If I didn't make sure that I was sharp and focused they simply didn't get in contact with me. I have quite a few therapists as my clients, and they complain that they haven't got any clients. I then have to get them to understand that they may be working with this for the wrong reasons. Contrary to most people within this line of work I would rather be without it. But it doesn't work like that. I'm not in this just for my *own* sake. And you might as well realize this since you are going to do it as well: this is just *a part* of your education.'

A new light appeared around him.

Then he said:

'Do not expect that they will set up a bust of you in the park. Do your work. Perform it with elegance and gratefulness. Never let yourself be misled by your vanity. Do not let yourself be led astray by romantic flattery or injured criticism from those who do not know better. It is not that you feel called – but you must simply follow your destiny. It is important to understand the difference. Be open and be always willing to learn. Be alert! – and that is it.'

The last sentence was underlined by a gentle pat on my knee with his fist:

'When, finally, a person is willing to step out of the mists of oblivion and has the courage to begin remembering, then this person will be recognized. Both up there and down here. When an individual remembers, he will be able to accept his task. Everybody has a task to perform here. And no one can fulfil someone else's purpose. That is why we may as well forget all about circumstances not being as good as they should be or that others have much better options than ourselves. The present circumstances are always the best possible at that moment. That's the way it is. If you cannot help yourself where you are right now, how could you possibly help others?'

The sun played peekaboo behind a cloud but disappeared quickly again. The Seer threw the rest of the water on the fire as a sign that it was time to start the work of the day. We helped each other to pack the equipment. We left the tent. I didn't think about that at the time, being occupied with all he had just said.

When we were ready, we stood for a moment inhaling the fresh air, the colours and the shapes coming to life in front of us. The sound of this silence was indescribable and yet it was only an overture to another kind of silence that was to come later, which must have been the most meaningful music on earth. We began ascending the east side of the mountain. The stronghold was further up.

The path was steep and difficult. On the mental plane it was clear that the Power was getting more and more intense and I could feel that something was pending. I sensed the activity in the ether around us. My joy was pure in a different way than before. It was not mushy, neither did it have its origin in any kind of sentimentality. Maybe that was the reason that I was more purely receptive. I did not consider the advantages of a simple life. At that moment I *was* that. I didn't long for anything. All that was needed was already in the game and within reach. Everything was contained in the breath. The joy had its root in gratitude: gratitude towards the Seer for having awakened me so effectively; gratitude towards the Power and the reality it made available; gratitude towards the great breath. All that I had always dreamt about but not really dared hope to regain. Never in my wildest dreams had I thought I would either deserve or be able to fulfil, because long ago I had once been unfaithful to it.

On a ledge on the other side a wild dog was watching us from the shadows of a thicket. As we got closer and stepped into the open it disappeared as silently as it had come.

It took us about an hour to climb the 200 metres. When we reached the top we took a short break in the ruins of an early settlement outside the stronghold. I had a single butterfly in my stomach as we walked along the wall towards the northern gate and the butterfly turned into many as we stepped into this holy place. The Seer, as usual, went to the middle of the courtyard. I followed him and, also as usual, stood at his right side.

The Seer drew an invisible circle on the ground with his stick. He stood stock still at the centre of the circle facing the tower of the stronghold to the northwest. In spite of his apparent immobility I saw him in his astral body. Here he was holding his arms stretched out to each side like wings and, slowly spinning about himself, he whirled faster and faster in a spiral-like vibration while the voice inside me chanted the following words in Aramaic:

'Ephatah! Ina na thar'a! – Ephatah! Ina na thar'a! – Ephatah! Ina na thar'a!'

(Open up! I am the door between the worlds!)

I stepped into the circle, which rotated faster and faster, drawing everything into it. All lines, all the corners of the world found their way towards this centripetal point of concentrated energy. I can only describe it like this: it was as if an intense suction was operating under the picture of the physical world turning it inside out. Thus, the ethereal vitality, hiding behind the apparent solidity of physical things, is made visible. This solidity is but one side of what we normally consider to be our reality. It is really just as natural as turning your jacket inside out, like pulling a veil aside. And in that same breath are all beings of light made visible.

Everything unfolds in an inexplicable silence, which is not the lack of sound but rather the consecration of it. If we consider the organ music of Bach to be the closest we can get to a reflection in sound of the ethereal filigree, and that the last string quartet of Beethoven is the closest we may get to the sound of human grief transformed into victory through the power of grace, then to my mind there is no contemporary music able to reflect the quietness I experienced here.

With my eyes closed a simple prayer surged through me:

Nehwey sibyanak aykana d'shmeya aph b'arah.

Let that happen on earth which is written among the stars.

Unfold the light of the universe through each of us in harmony with the universal laws.

I see that what is written among the stars is already unfolding on earth, because there is no difference between here and there. The ethereal reality is a far purer form of star-writing compared to the earthly one, a language which is not limited by gravity and Cronus.

Quiet – quiet – quiet – quiet – quiet – quiet . . . before my inner sight a small flame.

Then I hear the Voice – whispering in the wind:

    '*I was sent forth by the Power,*

    I have come to those who are able to receive me,

    I have been found by those who seek after me.

    Look upon me, you who wish to be united with me,

    Hear me, you who are listening.

    You, who are waiting for me, receive my essence.

    Forget me not!

    For I am the first and the last.

    I am the honoured one and the scorned one.

    I am the whore and the holy one.

    I am the wife and the virgin.

    I am the mother and the daughter.

    I am the celestial bride,

    For whom there is no husband.

    My power is from the one who sent me.

    I am the incomprehensible silence.

    I am the voice whose sound is manifold,

    And the word without end.

    I am the blessing of my name.

    I am wisdom and ignorance.

I am without shame and filled with it.
I am power, I am fear.
I am peace and war.
I am the void in fullness.
I am oneness in emptiness.
I dissolve all concepts.
Dissolve all images.
Thus, I am limitless.
Thus, I am all.
Forget me not,
Because I am the outcast and the long expected one.
Be vigilant, you who know how to listen,
Everyone who has been sent, listen,
Everyone who is now awake and resurrected from sleep.
Many are the pleasant forms making up the grand
    illusion,
The empty sin and transient desire,
Which humankind is embracing
Until they become spiritually sober
And go up to the appointed place.
That is where you will find me.
Then you shall live,
And never taste death again.'

The whispering voice speaks healingly to the innermost me, to the eternal being. Again and again I must give up the remainder of my resistance. What have I got to lose?

I am falling through an endless room. Then I am caught by unseen hands lifting me. What felt like gravity before is now transformed into grace – a quiet being in the breath of the universe. There is no separation, only healing and devotion.

It is a most touching sight and an indescribable condition as the field opens in a majestic movement and illuminates the whole courtyard. The light is so intense that I have to screw

up my eyes. The Seer is looking directly into it. I also look, and I see that it is Mariam, a radiating figure in front of us. The whole castle is surrounded by vibrations.

It is hard to know how long this continues. Time is without meaning. Then the symbol appears, pulsating in the intense light.

I am breathless and spellbound. Like last time, I feel compelled to step into this vibration and disappear into it. But the fear of not being able to live up to it keeps me back.

Suddenly I see it, the meaning of the symbol.

The two Mariam Magdalenes!

I open my eyes. I see two shadows on the ground in front of me – the Seer's and my own. Behind us the sun has broken through the ragged clouds. We are standing in the circle, side by side. I see the two women becoming clear in the sand and I realize that this is the sign of the Age of Aquarius. But that is not all. I also see that MM is the Roman numeral for 2000 – the new millennium.

I am totally speechless. Not only because of the unbelievable situation we are in, but also because of the significance of the secret language. The Seer is silent. The Voice is saying:

'Now you have seen it. But this is only the beginning. Remember, that what you have just witnessed is but a pale image of reality. Do not get lost in the images but concentrate all your power on the force behind them.'

'What is Mariam trying to tell us?' I asked the Seer.

'We'll see. Someone is trying to tell us something anyway. It is now our task to find out what it is.'

He stepped out of the circle. I stayed in the slipstream of the intense energy of the Power. The ethereal bubble in which I was standing yielded, and the elastic silver string connecting us slowly untied itself. A small, almost imperceptible snap followed by a faint sprinkling of small glowing particles rising in the air, and I looked at the white clouds in the sky drifting majestically like proud ships on an endless sea. That was all.

Liberated from all worries.

Being.

Later, when I had also stepped out of the circle and was sitting at the end of the courtyard, the Seer drew another circle around himself and slipped into the silence I had seen him practise so many times before. I sat watching him and got the urge to take a snapshot of him. I got out my camera and adjusted the lens. He was standing in the middle of the picture. The moment I pressed the release I saw, out of the corner of my eye, something to the left of the frame, something indefinable moving. I didn't think much about it until one month later when I had the film developed. To my great surprise I saw that the Seer was not alone in the picture of the courtyard, there was the image of a young man beside him.

When I had taken the picture and put the camera away I also fell silent. Except for the dancing energies around us only the Seer and I were present.

Imperceptibly I slid out of life's disguise, the body's frame, broke through the veil and floated upwards. My waves united with the waves of ether. I can see I am a life-giving energy and see that never has there been another separation than the one I myself have created with my inexplicably limited attitude and stubborn resistance. The ether is filled with radiating beings with small and almost invisible swirling particles of light. Indefatigable, present, maintaining, performing the eternal principle of creation.

'*The guardians of the fire!*' the Voice whispers.

Below me I saw a young man, the Silent One, squatting in one corner of the courtyard. The Seer called him over with an invisible sign. The Silent One got up and walked towards the radiating circle at the centre of the courtyard. The circle opened and I watched the two figures floating through unnumbered, nameless worlds.

Kansbar and Flegetanis.

I watched them walking across a sun-filled marketplace in Andalusia in another time. Nevertheless I sensed that what I was witnessing was also happening in the eternal now. It has happened before. It is happening now. And it shall happen again. Until the task has been fulfilled these two souls shall float through the worlds passing on the baton until they meet and recognize each other for what they really are.

'Who is this white-bearded Kansbar?'

At a railway station several centuries later the Seer passes on an age-old manuscript into the care of the Silent

One. Shortly after, the train with the Silent One and the manuscript disappears into one of the timeless tunnels of reality. The Silent One goes home and writes a book about his encounter with eternity.

'But who is Kansbar?'

All the thoughts and actions of humanity throughout time are stored in the ethereal – Akasha. Everything. Every little bit. Every *yod*!

Through our thoughts and actions we create our reality ourselves. Reality is exactly as limited or unlimited as we make it. I see that the human being is a transformer. We transform matter and the heavy dead weight of form into live energy. If we choose to.

If we choose not to, we remain petrified, guards and prisoners.

We have neglected our work here for far too long and filled the ether with unreflected, unchanged, heavy and dark matter. Filled it with all our untamed desires and projections. Through thousands of years we have developed very slowly. It has happened according to the principle of two steps forward and one back. Sometimes even one step forward and two back.

We have been the prisoners and guards of heavy matter and form for far too long. As if we have completely forgotten who we are, where we come from and what wonderful possibilities and abilities we possess.

But we have now passed quarter day. From now on we shall no more be asked. We may choose to accept the transformation or not. But it happens now. Not tomorrow in some obscure Nirvana, but HERE AND NOW! Nirvana is here now! Shamballa is here now! Heaven is here now! There shall not be other circumstances better than those we are in now. I see this now, and now I do understand.

We can transform the choking illusions of property rights and monopoly into a liberation of philanthropy and service. We can change fear into joy only when we let go of our stubborn insistence on being the chosen ones and being more special than other people. This is the only real way in which to be unique.

We can transform any kind of power and see how limited, how totally ridiculous and unimportant it is. We can transform imprisonment to freedom, separation to unity, disease to wholeness. If we choose to.

Death is like walking through a door from one room to another. There is no death, if we decide it. Death is something we have created in the ignorance of fear, in the unconscious race of galloping worries. We are killing ourselves with all our limited fantasies of what happiness is – our dreams about this and that, cars, money, luxuries, the perfect partner, perfect surroundings, perfect conditions. The perfect guru. The perfect sexuality. The perfect spirituality. Anything. The dream about being something special. This trap is wide open and springs again and again every time another poor fellow is trapped. Man is killing himself with the fear of losing all that, even before he has greedily sunk his neurotic claws into it.

Forget it.

Rise up. Take up your bed and walk – you are healed.

Rise up. Take responsibility for yourself.

If you choose to.

'Who can make themselves the judge of others?'

The Voice is a part of the ethereal. It speaks to me and still I am that Voice.

'When someone judges others, she or he is judging themselves.'

I am weightless and present everywhere. This is everywhere and nowhere. A non-local being. The moment the

Voice shapes its acknowledgement, that presents itself as words, but is, in reality, holy sound, any kind of judgement is silenced, because then everything becomes whole and reality is without opposites.

Without reservation, I now see the busy agents of ether, created by all our fearful thought forms. These agents, as opposed to the maintaining and healing beings of light, are undermining and separating. Nevertheless, there is no difference between them as such. They are the two sides to every question, an expression of our choices and thus the will of eternity.

How can I see and acknowledge all that when at the same time I realize that I am just a cosmic baby who hasn't even learned to walk yet?

All my being is one big question floating in ether through the universes. I wonder if it shall ever understand that the answer is to be found within itself?

'Areyoubeginningtounderstandinwhatmultidimensional reality we exist?'

The figure of the Seer stood in front of me, outlined against the sun.

'You have seen something of the things awaiting you. Seen some of the possibilities you may access as a human being.'

I nodded and looked around. Green ivy was crawling over the wall of the stronghold. The release of a camera clicked. I looked towards the sound and thought that I saw a figure moving. But no one was there. I heard the Voice behind me:

'It is time for you to take the next step. You shall learn which principles are the basis for moving about freely and consciously in ethereal reality.'

For a moment I was paralysed between two types of consciousness. On one side the Seer who had brought me here, on the other – the Voice:

'An individual enters the world as an empty cup. This emptiness is filled with a creative silence. Certainty lives in this silence. The certainty about humanity's innate, eternal nature. Certainty is without words and ideas. It has no need for explanations. It just is. Humanity is not allowed to remain in this state for long. From the time of birth the surroundings immediately begin to fill this apparent void with noise and with lessons, in order for an individual to learn how to relate to the external world, learn how to walk, how to talk, how to become a social being. It is a shame, however, that in that process humans forget all about the original certainty of the void. Instead of finding the equilibrium of options you lose yourself one-sidedly in the external world. Until the day when the cup has been filled to the brim with noise and lies, you get ill or somehow are forced to re-evaluate your life.'

I thought about the Sufis, the mystics dressed in white, known as the mystical side of Islam. They use a term called 'unlearning' or 'emptying the cup'. So that, once more, there will be room for silence and certainty.

The Voice continued:

'Without a creative silence there is no way that you'll be able to take one single step towards release and liberation. Without it, all aspirations to gain enlightenment will be more or less wasted. When the cup has been emptied and silence restored, there is no use for aspirations. No more will there be any talk about forward or backward. No more will there be stagnation. Humanity is what it always was: moving, creative silence. The difference between the one state and the other is simply that in silence you are awake and creative, and you know that it is so. In a state of noise you are more or less a sleeping zombie in the world. A zombie with lots of nonsensical actions that humans have made into the mantra of their lives.'

The words did not in the least sound strange to me. I was very well aware that it was not only a mental understanding but a total transformation that was awaiting.

The Seer stepped in front of me:

'But before you may start this process you must have the courage to face what in some traditions is called *The Guardian of the Threshold*, the necessary acknowledgement with the most cleansing effect. That is, if the process is successful. Tonight you'll sleep in the tent on the mountain slope. This is something you must go through on your own.'

He was watching the mountain. Then he hummed a line from a song the title of which I do not remember any more. He turned around and started walking. I watched him disappear.

If possible, it was even more difficult moving down than up. It was almost as if the narrow, impassable path wanted to underscore the Seer's sarcastic motto, 'Why go down when you can go up.'

Struggling to keep my balance on the way down I was suddenly struck by faint-heartedness. I was on another path than the one we had used climbing up. Hoping that it would take me to the tent I continued. It was a cul-de-sac. I looked in vain for the tent further down but couldn't see it. Arms held me tightly as I fought to get free of the thicket on my way down to our starting point. But where was it? For a moment I was seized by panic. Where did my feeling of 'walking on safe ground' suddenly disappear to? Where had my newly found knowledge of the connection between all things gone to? Why did I lose my pluck just because I met a little resistance? At this exact moment my foot slipped on a stone and I went over the edge. I rolled down the mountain side for endless seconds, through thickets and over rocks. In a last desperate attempt to break my fall I succeeded in catching hold of a small tree, which bent dangerously under the weight of this new and unexpected burden. I lay quite still in order to catch my breath. The tent was positioned on the ledge below me.

'Pride comes before a fall!' a tiny voice whispered.

The earth turned until the sun had disappeared behind the snow-covered Pyrenees. I sat by the fire tending to a few cuts, but I couldn't really concentrate on the matter at hand. The valley and its nature, which normally had an enchanting effect on me, had totally lost their attraction. I thought that I might just have lost my ability to appreciate all this beauty. Everything was just a surface. Devilishly beautiful settings created by just as devilish forces. An empty kind of beauty without any other purpose than that of beauty. And the emptiness was monumental. I pricked up my ears. Forced myself to listen, but not a sound. The silence wasn't even there. No birds were singing. No wind was moving. Everything seemed lifeless. Even the last rays of the sun seemed colourless. Darkness came creeping. I told myself that I could feel its cold essence and was seized by an inexplicable negative sensation. I hurriedly threw the last of the brushwood onto the fire, crawled into the tent, zipped the opening to behind me and crept into my sleeping bag. The flames danced a dance of shadows on the tent canvas. Even now as I sit here writing about it I feel the fear almost as I felt it then. I can feel the emptiness surrounding me then. An incomprehensible isolation from the rest of creation. And I saw how insignificant a man can be. How insignificant most of what was me really was compared to everything else.

The dancing shadows disappeared and I was swallowed up by darkness. An isolated thought of fear wrapped in the great nothingness. A nothingness in the merciless emptiness of the dark. Within this thought I saw everything I had done. The unbelievable suffering I had put others through time after time. I saw how all my thoughts, the lust, the failures, the ambitions and actions, conscious as well as unconscious, had left situations and whole worlds in an inconceivable and fatal chaos. The thought seemed to contract in the darkness. Became a particle, a centre of unfathomable weight, the only content of which was sin! The moment I realized that this particle of sin was me, the world disappeared from under me and I fell down and down further. At the same moment I also realized that this sin grew from the sickness in my mind, that the sin and the disease were one and the same, and that I would forever be trapped in this terrible limitation. Desperately, I reached into the darkness to find something to hold on to. But nothing was there. My cries were sucked into this nothingness without a sound. I fell and fell while the centre became more and more dense and heavier.

'Help me! Save me! Forgive me!' I begged.

But there was no answer because there was no one there to answer me.

Was this the eternal darkness into which only the ultimately lost souls are thrown, eternal perdition where there is no pardon and no forgiveness?

'*Yes,*' the small voice said.

The centre grew heavier and expanded suddenly, while the speed was now so high that I just hoped this endless darkness would after all come to an end, that it would have a bottom against which this terrible weight would be crushed and forever disappear. Instead, I experienced the centre growing at an increasing speed, that, so to speak, it grew into the darkness so that there was no difference between them. The centre and the darkness were one. I was no longer a specific centre in that emptiness. I was this darkness. The sum total of all that is immovable, all that is unreleased and unchanged, tied down to eternal limitations.

In the middle of all this I suddenly realized that the terrible fall had come to an end. My essence was gravity and space but the downward movement had stopped. There was no movement at all. I was, so to speak, caught within myself. The knowledge about the only alternative to this seemingly finite nightmare made the situation impossible. And worst of all, memory. My memory about former, wasted possibilities burning into my centre like an eternal fire without leaving a single ray of light. Damnation was total. And there was only myself to thank. This acknowledgement was made with my last remaining resources as if I had only been allotted so much potential. But exactly my potential – my memory was my remaining chance of salvation. I was hanging on the utmost edge of the chasm of oblivion with my fingertips, clinging on to my last ray of hope when an almost invisible, radiating

Hazrat Inayat Khan (1882–1927)
(Photo: Sikar van Stolk)

spot appeared like a mirage in nothingness. I was about to let go of everything when in that radiating spot I thought that I recognized a face. I concentrated in order to see who it was. Slowly, the face grew clearer and I could feel how this wonderful miracle restored my powers. I could now see who it was. Hazrat Inayat Khan, my old sufi master, whose book, *Gayan, Vadan, Nirtan* had been sent to me anonymously, when at 15 years old I found myself in a deep crisis. Hazrat Inayat Khan whose teachings had meant so much to me and, of this I had always been certain, had guided me from the beyond. He now appeared on this my judgement day. Tears rolled down my cheeks. At that moment the face changed and I recognized one of the many people who had supported me on my way through life. And I saw the long row of people to whom I now knew I owed everything. If all these souls had not existed for me, I would have perished long ago. The face changed once more and was now so close that I could feel its imperishable force. The smile of the white-bearded Seer with his deep blue eyes was standing in front of me. Then I let go and felt how I was lifted up, up and up while the darkness slowly changed into light.

I have the old, timeless manuscript, which was given to me by the Seer, in front of me. I realize that it has always followed me. Every time I lose sight of it the One Dressed in White comes forward. Sometimes as Kansbar, other times as a voice in my heart. At times, when I open the manuscript, the letters turn into signs, and I do not know what they mean. At other times the words dance towards me like well-known beings of light, singing, opening doors to worlds I didn't even know existed. I turn another page and read.

6

Mariam lifted her head towards the sound. She caught a glimpse of a platform at the end of the hall. On this platform was a throne. She was surrounded on all sides by a colourful, ornate and foreign script. Her eyes hauntedly swept over the wall in a desperate attempt to read the writing, but all she found was an indefinable echo in the furthermost nooks and crannies of her mind – memory. A soft wind made waves of parts of the wall. Then she remembered.

The Temple of Isis.

The waving wall was pulled aside. A figure, with an enormous ox mask pulled over his head and upper part of his body, stepped in. A sundial was placed over the horns with a snake in front of it. The figure mounted the raised platform and sat down on the throne.

'Mariam, daughter of Isis. The hall you are in is the first

sphere of the divine mind, which is matter. The divine mind is without beginning and without end. This transient world is just one of the many ideas of the divine mind. It is within this mind that man breathes, lives and *is*. When the student has gained the right to carry the Key of the Master and is able to open the many doors of the mental and psychic rooms of the Temple of Wisdom and enter them free and wise, the principles behind the concepts of energy, power and matter shall be revealed as well as the necessary knowledge of how to handle them. The one who understands the truth behind the mental nature of the universe has already come a long way towards mastery. But it is impossible to reach the goal without the Key of the Master.'

Mariam was standing in front of the throne with her eyes closed while the words of the priest enveloped her. When she decided to open her eyes again she was very surprised to find that she was now standing in a cloister garden surrounded by rose bushes. In the middle of the garden a loaf of bread was rising in the morning sun on a stone altar.

I am only a thought, she thought. All things around me are simply the thoughts of the Sublime One expressed in matter. This is the endless song that God is singing. One verse after the other. A poem of creation in which everything is made concurrently with the ability of the waiting darkness to hear it. Let me be the most insignificant *yod*, the most humble of the written characters, in this song. The smallest echo of the great silence.

Everything was predestined. Nothing happened haphazardly. Mariam knew what she had to do and stepped in front of the stone altar in the middle of the garden. She stayed in the same spot all day long watching the imperceptible transformation of the dough into bread. When the sun set the bread was done.

Mariam's days were lonely days. The lessons continued without any breaks. The Hall of the Ox became her prison. Only god knows how many times she witnessed the creation of bread by the sun. *The oven of the soul*!

She vaguely remembered events which gave her an insecure feeling that something was missing. But she didn't remember what it was.

From time to time, the monotony was broken. She started counting the days. She had a day off every seven days. On those days she stayed in her cell and the enclosed garden belonging to it. For 153 days she didn't see any other novices.

Then suddenly one day a change occurred. Early one morning she was collected by two veiled women leading her through unknown passages and into a magnificent bath. She sensed the admiration and envy of the two women when they undressed her and were confronted with her youthful beauty. They disappeared when they had finished bathing her and Mariam was left in the care of a black woman who didn't try to hide her admiration for the unique being who had been given into her temporary care. She immediately began her work.

Mariam was told to lie down on a couch and the woman started removing all unwanted hair from Mariam's body with a sharp knife. Mariam reluctantly followed the woman's actions. When she gently wanted to force her legs apart Mariam protested and held her knees together. But the woman smiled firmly and pushed Mariam back onto the couch, and with a firm grip she forced her legs apart. She lay immovable in fear of the sharp edge of the knife, but the woman worked with very careful and distinct movements clearly demonstrating that she had done this many times before. When the intimate process was over and the woman had made sure that it was done properly, she started massaging

Mariam with ethereal oils. The black hands moved with slow, intense movements over the tense body. Without any shame they kept circling the most sensitive spots, and Mariam felt how a secret fire was lit and spread its burning sensuality under the thin skin of her body. She wanted to resist her, but the black woman simply looked at her in a way that made her give up any further resistance.

As if in a languorous dance the woman led Mariam slowly but firmly into a foreign country where a totally new power ruled. A power which was about to explode in her womb at any moment.

No matter how hard she fought against it in her mind she finally gave in totally to her repressed desires so that when the woman stopped, leaving her a pliant victim gasping for air, Mariam wanted the woman to go on with her treatment. Instead, the woman helped Mariam to her feet. She could barely stand on her own. Electric currents rushed through her shining body.

Before she knew it two female slaves were dressing her in a light gown made from a transparent material, which, although covering her body, clearly emphasized her nakedness. Finally, they combed Mariam's hair and covered her face with the sign of the dancer, the provocative half-moon veil.

They led her through dimly lit passages until they stood in front of a striped curtain. Only when she found herself standing in a room without any visible walls did she see that it was the Hall of the Ox, but that they had arrived through the entrance usually used by the teacher.

In the middle of the hall on a platform that she hadn't noticed before was an enormous bridal couch already prepared, surrounded by a sea of oil lamps. The slaves pushed her closer and she saw that a young man was waiting on the bed. It was not until she was standing at the foot of the bed that she noticed that the handsome boy was naked. He smiled shyly at the sight of Mariam and he reacted quite naturally. She turned her eyes away from his erect member but felt a strong compulsion to let herself slide down on the inviting bed. The entire hall was enveloped in a warm, vibrating light and she could hardly stand on her feet. She was about to give in when a pair of hands took a firm grip around her arms and held her like a vice. Out of the corner of her eye she saw a small wooden phallus hastily being smeared with a kind of shiny liniment. The smell was putrid. It was henbane.

Before Mariam was able to register what was going to happen, the hands forced her to bend over, and other hands forced the smeared wooden phallus into her from behind. The action was unexpected and the pain so sharp that she was paralysed by it. The hands held her firmly until the herbal liniment started to work. Then they slowly pulled the instrument out of her and let her go.

As if in a dream Mariam floated through the air towards the young boy who pulled her into a warm embrace. Without any resistance she opened her mouth and let him kiss her deeply and for a long time. Hands moved over her stomach and suddenly she felt them all over her body until she lifted her buttocks from the bed and bent like a bow pressing her abdomen against the youngster. Never before had she felt anything like this. The young man lifted her up and together they rode through torn landscapes of deep longing. She felt that she was being severed and that the slow ride filled her totally to the point where the pain disappeared into unknown horizons far from time and place. Again the hands seized her and the young man turned her over, and trembling he entered her once more. Now the rhythm changed. Faster and faster they rode through a somewhat heavier landscape where pain and pleasure fused into an inseparable unity. She opened her eyes in order to look into the eyes of her lover in this moment of ecstasy.

Her scream disappeared in the noise from the rhythmic chanting of the surrounding crowd. Above her an enormous shadow with the head of an ox moved back and forth, back and forth, harder and harder until she lost consciousness and let herself be swallowed up by a distant and cool peacefulness.

'What is she doing here?'

A masterful woman's voice reached her from far away.

'She is among the chosen ones,' another woman with a more primitive dialect replied.

Mariam opened her eyes slightly. Against the light she saw a tall, beautiful woman dressed in the gown of Those Dressed in White. The woman came to the couch where Mariam was lying. Mariam immediately closed her eyes when the cover was removed from her body. In a desperate attempt to shield her nakedness she turned on her side and covered herself with her hands.

'Lie still!' the voice with the primitive dialect commanded her.

'Let her be.'

Mariam felt a gentle hand on her shoulder turning her over until she was lying on her back again.

'Do not be afraid. My name is Salome. This is not the first time that I have seen a beautiful young girl without her clothes, but never have I seen anyone as beautiful as you.'

Mariam opened her eyes fully and stared into the most enchanting eyes she had ever seen. The woman again covered Mariam's body and turned her attention to the other woman at the end of the couch:

The Synagog
(W Hegeb & W Pinder)

'Atuka liked that, eh? The first one to pick this rare flower. How far is he with his preparations?'

The other woman, whom Mariam could now see was a black slave, turned her eyes away without answering.

'You heard me, how far is he?'

The female slave clearly felt ill at ease. She was embarrassed and twisted and turned uncomfortably. Salome's eyes flashed. She looked questioningly at Mariam but realized at the same moment that she couldn't expect an answer from her.

The black slave broke down crying as Salome took hold of her. It was obvious that the patience of the Woman Dressed in White was at an end:

'Is it so that he has already picked it?' she cried.

The slave was shaking. She fell to the floor and still crying she tried to explain. But Salome no longer had any doubt about the answer. For a brief moment Mariam's and Salome's eyes met and the former sensed in her drowsiness the mixture of hurt and anger in the dark eyes.

The One Dressed in White reached out towards her with one hand:

'Let's get out of here.'

The women rode north. They followed the roads along the river on the first day, but after two days of riding Salome led them across the north-eastern corner of Wadi Natrun. They did not talk much but Mariam's memory became clearer with every hour that passed. She rocked gently along in her saddle and surrendered unconditionally to the safety and strength radiating from her liberator in white. Now and again they would stop to drink. Salome handed Mariam a piece of bread, which she kept in her saddlebag. She herself didn't eat anything.

'Cover yourself against the wind and the sun,' she said when in the middle of the day they were crossing the desert.

Endless expanses of sand and impassable plains full of rocks stretched out in front of them, and when the wind started to blow they struggled forward step by step. However, it did not take long before the hardships were behind them. The landscape changed and became lush and fertile. Now and again they would see other travellers, and the closer they got to the coast the more travellers they met. Salome stopped on a hill and pointed to a town in the distance:

'This is Alexandria, the centre of wisdom and science.'

She hesitated for a while but then continued:

'Unfortunately, it is also that of fools.'

She smiled at Mariam and a little while later she chuckled away in a low and catching laugh, which made Mariam want to join in. It was a laughter that she would hear many times and that she would come to love.

Salome now pointed to the right of the town:

'This is the lake of Mareotis. This is where we are going. Let us not waste any more time.'

Late in the day they rode into the jungle growth of a forest surrounding the lake that Salome had pointed out earlier. Coming out on the other side, to her great astonishment Mariam saw a series of buildings of a kind she had never seen before. The houses were identical, white with various symbols painted on them and situated in a kind of cluster but still with a fair distance between them. In the middle of the formation a slightly larger house was situated.

Salome headed for a house on the outskirts of the cluster.

'Welcome to the *Therapeutae*,' she said smilingly to Mariam.

Goats were grazing inside fences and all kinds of medicinal herbs were growing around and on the walls of the houses. Mariam was met by the smell of hyssop as she entered Salome's house.

Behind the living room two smaller rooms were situated. Salome showed Mariam into one of them:

'This is yours. We cannot know for how long you are going to stay. But it is important that you get plenty of rest and get well. It will take a few days before you recover from the effects of Atuka's magical drink.'

A dust-filled ray of light danced in the opening of the window and crawled along the clay wall. Mariam stayed in her bed listening to the sound of distant bells. She stretched lazily and yawned from wellbeing, got up and stood enjoying the fresh air in front of the open window. A flock of goats were on their way down the slopes toward the lake eating the juicy grass on the way. Mariam took a deep breath of fresh air and felt a rush of inexplicable happiness suffuse her. So this was the paradise of Those Dressed in White. The Society of Therapists to borrow Salome's expression.

'Good to see you up and about.'

Salome stood smiling in the doorway.

'Come outside. I have prepared some food for you. When you have eaten you must tell me everything.'

They sat down on benches in a small courtyard in front of the house. Mariam dined in silence but Salome didn't have anything.

'Now tell me,' Salome said when Mariam had finished eating.

And Mariam told her everything that she had experienced. She told her about the strange vision in the washhouse in her home in Bethany, about the omen which had come true, about the terrible death of her parents, about her betrothal and her husband-to-be whom she had hardly seen. She told her about Lazarus, her brother, about the Brotherhood and the dramatic journey to the temple of Heliopolis, about the experience with the charismatic Helen and meeting the old white-haired woman who had appeared from nowhere to guide her and who had disappeared just as unnoticed again.

The sun was setting when Mariam ended her story. Salome sat with a familiar smile on her face, while she silently nodded as though everything Mariam told her simply confirmed something she already knew. They sat for a while in silence.

In this silence Mariam felt that her story brought up numerous questions to which there were no answers and she was suddenly seized by strong doubts about her own credibility. Had she just imagined all of it? Had she merely experienced a completely different kind of magic drink than she had been given in Heliopolis?

'Do not despair.'

It was Salome who broke Mariam's strange series of thoughts.

'Everything you have experienced, everything you saw and everything that happened are real events. There might still be things you do not understand, but before long you'll see that they are all elements of a greater plan.'

She looked intensely at Mariam as if she had seen something that even Mariam herself hadn't seen. Something deep in her soul which had not been wakened yet and which was waiting in the dark for its release.

'I have been waiting a long time for this day. It almost went wrong, but luckily I was informed in the nick of time about your presence at the Temple of Isis. And now you are here.'

Mariam listened. Then she said:

'I thought that it had been decided that I should go to Heliopolis to study. It seemed natural. During the whole journey I was assisted by the Brotherhood. All had been planned. It was written.'

Salome interrupted her:

'Nothing is written.'

The words were neither hard nor reserved but they brought something else into the conversation.

'The Brotherhood is so many things. There are more sections. Some of them are not in contact with the powers that they boast about in all humility. We are working with a small group under the Essenes at the Carmel Mountain but lately our work has been made difficult. Another group, which has settled down at the Dead Sea want to protect their own interests.'

'Who and what is this Brotherhood?'

'Their doctrines are age-old. The patriarchs secretly brought the written law along from Babylon when the people were released from captivity. Back in Jerusalem it came to a confrontation when the group of scribes and scholars, who tried to start a new spiritual basis for the rebuilding of the nation, disagreed. The final result was that two groups, the Pharisees and the Sadducees, formed a governing power structure, while a third group, the Essenes, withdrew and disappeared into the periphery where they continued the original teachings about the simple life. This group settled on Mount Carmel where it has resided ever since. Since then, however, a dispute started within the Brotherhood. The bases for all the groups are the teachings of Enoch, Isaiah, Hosea, Micah and the traditions of Nahum. They look upon themselves as the people who must pave the way for the coming of the Messiah. Among them are scholars of great wisdom, scholars supplying the world with prophecies of great beauty. They have a proud tradition of maintaining and passing on the scriptures. Some of them are seers and very adept healers. Their weakness lies in the fact that they have been faced with a splitting up of the groups, which has led some of them astray.'

'How have they been led astray?'

'Well, they scorn women. They are banned from the Holy of Holies but are most mercifully allowed to do the chores that have always been the burden of women. One of the groups alone, the Nazarenes (the Consecrated Ones), living at Capernaum on the banks of the Sea of Galilee, have opened their community to women. That one still has a connection to the Carmel group whereas the groups at Damascus, the Dead Sea and Beersheba work separately. Here they totally deny the power between the sexes. They are strictly celibate.'

Mariam was looking at Salome while she talked. She managed, however, to get a few words in:

'Are they also called "Those Dressed in White?"'

Salome smiled:

'There is quite a confusion about that among outsiders who respect the Brotherhood very much, because they are always hospitable, always ready to help and offer any kind of medical aid that may be needed. As you can see, we are all dressed in white, but this doesn't necessarily mean that we share the views of the Brotherhood.'

Now Mariam looked confused and Salome laughed out loud. Then she explained.

'I understand your confusion. Ages ago a small group of men and women arrived in the Holy Land from the east. The group was called *Kamal Posh*. It means something like '*those who dress in blankets*'. Each member owned just one blanket, which they wore during the day and slept under during the night. They very quickly got the name '*Those Dressed in White*', since the blankets they wore were usually white. No one knew where they came from. They simply arrived one day bringing with them a profound wisdom, which they began teaching to those who wished to receive it. They possessed the gifts of Heaven and legend tells us there was no disease that they could not heal. They made prophecies and could see further and deeper than the most esteemed prophets and seers of the time. Their renown went far and wide, and as often happens in such cases their abilities caused a lot of envy among those who ruled the country and who did not understand that it was possible to possess such abilities without wanting to usurp their power. Thus the sect was persecuted and forced to hide in the mountains. As the years went by a small society developed and the members began writing down the secrets of the teaching. The Brotherhood or the Essenes originate from this group of people just like we Therapists do. As you see, our gowns are also white, and they always have been. In our society both men and women may be accepted. Some of them are even married.'

Mariam collected her thoughts after Salome's explanation. She had never heard about the Therapists before.

'What is the task of the Therapists?'

'That is a long story. Hopefully, we are just a passing phenomenon. Unfortunately, it looks as if this interim is going to last longer than expected. We pass on knowledge. We initiate people who are ready to be initiated into the heavenly secrets. We heal and make prophecies just as our predecessors did. On top of that we also master all the languages and most of the dialects.'

She fell silent and looked at Mariam. Then she continued:

'But my greatest task is . . . you!'

Mariam looked at her open-mouthed.

'Me?'

'Yes, you.'

Now Salome was laughing again as if this laughter was a companion to everything she said and only needed the slightest reason to break through. It was like small bells sounding in the air and reverberating and transforming everything that had formerly been locked, into a liberating ethereal dance. But there were still quite a few things to which Mariam needed an answer.

'How did you know that I was in Heliopolis?'

Salome turned serious again:

'Who do you think led you through the desert and led you away from your guards the evening you were getting in trouble?'

Mariam sat for a while thinking.

'You mean the cloaked one?'

'The cloaked one, well, why not? It certainly was a young woman dressed in our gown and leading the way on her donkey.'

'A woman?'

Mariam's bewilderment increased.

'Of course. Didn't you think that a woman could endure such hardship? You must have forgotten all the things you yourself have been through. Do you remember anything from your time in the temple?'

Mariam searched her memory but didn't get any further than the moment when she happily arrived at the temple and drank from the cup, which was to become a daily ritual and which dissolved any sense of context.

'I remember the animals. Strange beasts with animal heads and two legs. Everything is like a dream. Well, I do remember opening my eyes and seeing you for the first time.'

Salome was silent for a while, wondering whether or not to tell Mariam the truth. Mariam broke the silence:

'What happened there? I know that it wasn't a very nice place, but . . .'

Salome gently interrupted her:

'The Temple of Isis is not what it used to be. If the families who send their daughters to this place knew what is going on, they would break it down immediately. Atuka is a degenerate soul who has created his own little kingdom within the temple walls. Under cover of training temple virgins and supplying initiations to hopeful novices he, instead, takes advantage of them and molests them for his devious purposes. If the families knew . . .'

It was now Mariam's turn to interrupt:

'What purposes?'

Salome wanted to ignore the question but something in Mariam's eyes made her realize that the girl in front of her was made of the same material as she was herself. This realization filled her with a quiet happiness. She let go of her reservation and said:

'The lust of the flesh. Atuka takes advantage of the girls. And the boys as well for that matter. Credible witnesses who have been lucky enough to get away have told about all the despicable things going on there.'

'How did you succeed in getting me out?'

'We have connections everywhere. People we may rely on. You have been on my mind for a long time. Well, actually for many years. When I heard that you had arrived at the Temple of Isis I knew that I had to act. Unfortunately, it took me a few months before I gained access to the temple. The novice doesn't get more freedom of movement until she has been through the introductory tests and initiations or whatever they call it.'

'Was I initiated then?'

Salome had to smile, but she also saw that there was no getting around it.

'Apparently.'

'What went on during the initiation?'

Persian dervish/Kamal Posh
(India Office Collections circa 1890)

'It is hard to say in your case but from what we hear Atuka's rituals of initiation are – shall we say – of a sort of promiscuous kind.'

'You mean he rapes the virgins?'

'Well, yes.'

Mariam shivered. The sun had disappeared behind the horizon and it had grown cool. They went in. Salome lit the fire and continued talking about it in a most natural manner:

'It wasn't you who got raped in the Temple of Isis, it was your body. Even Atuka cannot touch your soul. You were not even there when the so-called initiation took place. Some day you'll remember where you travelled in spirit.'

'How did this Atuka manage to mislead the Brotherhood?'

'The Brotherhood shuts its eyes to the debauchery going on behind the walls because they thus escape responsibility for the female novices by leaving them to him. The temples in Heliopolis rest on an almost indestructible reputation going as far back as the time of Moses. And as long as the virgins may be trained in the Temple of Isis, the Brotherhood does not have to send them into the arms of the priests of the Pharisees and the Sadducees in Jerusalem. This last would be a thorn in the flesh of the zeal of the Brotherhood. As you can see, as long as Atuka works with the blessing of the Brotherhood, he may do more or less as he pleases. You are not the first one that I have brought out from places like this.'

'Who else?'

'You'll learn soon enough. Some day you may even meet some of them. But now we must call it a day.'

Salome got up and lit two big candles on an altar-like table. She then sat down with her legs crossed and said:

'You are welcome to take part in this ritual. Let it be your first step on this new path.'

Mariam sat down in the same manner and Salome started uttering the words that would follow Mariam for the rest of her life just like Salome's laughter:

'Heavenly Source,
You who are everywhere,
Hallowed be Thy name.
Thy Kingdom come,
Thy will be done here and now in all eternity.
Fill us with the power of Thy grace,
And free us from the chains with which we bind each
        other.
Lead us out of temptation: Free us from ourselves,
And lend us the power to be one with You.
Teach us the true power of forgiveness,
May this holy moment be the ground
From which all our future actions grow.
Amen.'

7

In the quietness, I just lay there and watched the early morning light through the canvas of the tent. Then I remembered the events of the night and felt how, quite remarkably, I was filled with a new kind of courage. There was a totally new and almost unreal quality in me, which I had never known before. It was a kind of reality that seemed more real than anything I had known earlier. Something had changed. Quietly I got to my knees and crawled outside.

The air around me was crystal clear – and I now saw that it consisted of innumerable, small, pulsating crystal-like beings mirroring each other and connected by fine threads, *nadis* of radiant light. Carefully I reached out in order to caress this eternal filigree and felt a faint, vibrating sensation on my skin. It almost felt like taking the pulse of another person.

A pulsating being, a being of light without any identity, drew a radiant line in the air in the same way that I once saw the Seer doing it, but which he never explained to me.

'One thing is to be able to see and sense this light. Another thing is to be able to concentrate the ethereal energy and for a moment to apply it with a healing purpose. In order to do that you must bring the level of vibration into harmony with that of the universe in which you want to work, or the level on which you want to work. No more and no less. If you are too slow you drop the energy on the floor so to speak – if you are too fast you may easily miss the target. It demands precision and a willpower of such magnitude that it is freed from any desire of power and wish to feel special. Your power must be in harmony with that of the universe. It doesn't want anything for itself. It doesn't owe anything to anyone and isn't owed anything either. It is neutral but in a compassionate way. Call it respect for life. And yet, it is more of a new understanding of the reality and the circumstances in which humanity finds itself at the moment.'

A radiant heart was hanging two metres up in the air. There was nothing mysterious about the sight. It seemed quite natural. It was just another step on my path, a new door opening through this image and speaking to me from the deepest of layers.

Above the heart I saw a pyramid turned upside down. The triangle was made from the fire that is never quenched and the water from which all higher life springs through the initiations of the mystics. A symbol which I knew to be the symbol of the Heavenly Source, the Creator, the Father/Mother, radiated from the top left edge of the triangle.

The symbol of the Heavenly Child, the Created, the Son/Daughter radiated from the top right edge of the triangle.

The symbol of *Rukha d'koodsha*, the Holy Spirit, radiated from the lower point of the triangle. At the same time, the whole triangle symbolized the three uppermost energy centres of the human being: the crown centre, brow centre and throat centre.

Below the heart was an upright pyramid. This triangle was filled with earthly fire and the water from which transient life arises.

The masculine symbol radiated from the bottom left edge and the feminine from the right one.

The symbol of *Naphsha,* the Higher Self, humanity's connection upwards, the bridge to the higher worlds, radiated from the topmost point. Within this triangle the human being's lower centres of energy were represented, the root, sacral and solar plexus centres.

Both triangles slowly glided towards the heart. The upper triangle more or less floated down from the sky while the lower one, so to speak, rose from the dead. As the triangles united and embraced the heart, all the symbols became one symbol containing all. All the qualities were expressed in this hexagon floating and vibrating in the air. I felt the certainty in my heart at the moment the sign became whole.

I do not know how long this went on. Whether it lasted for a moment or for an eternity, what's the difference? At a deeper level, however, I had no doubt what all this was about. The Star with the heart was the sign of Mariam Magdalene – the sign of the cosmic, feminine power. At this time I had no idea that there were others who had similar experiences. At that time, I was unaware of the extent to which the Magdalene archetype had been opening up with the collective unconscious and that others, each in their own way, were drawing on the same source. On another level this had something to do with my future relationship with the Seer, in the same way it had to do with my work, which I was just then beginning to sense and which I have since had to take upon me because it is mine.

I sat and immediately wrote down the details of my experience in my notebook and thought about the road that had led me to this event, the basic principle that had started me on this path.

It was not until 1989 that I really began to recognize Mariam Magdalene's rightful place in Christian mythology. My studies in early Christian and Gnostic writings told a story about a woman and a being that spoke directly to something deep inside me. I tried to describe Mariam's physical appearance to the Danish painter Hans Krull who was inspired to produce a number of watercolour paintings and etchings of her. A few years later I made a very surprising discovery. One of my friends sent me an Italian postcard of Leonardo Da Vinci's *The Last Supper*: a picture that many of us know so well that we do not really see it properly. The postcard became a bookmark in one of the books I was reading. It was not until later, when I picked up the book again, that I noticed a curious detail in the painting for the first time. Leonardo's painting was of Yeshua and the twelve disciples at the last supper, that is, thirteen men. However, the person who caught my eye in the painting was indisputably a woman. She sat at the right hand of Yeshua, beautiful, shy and leaning away from him. There was no doubt that this person was a woman and this woman was Mariam Magdalene.

The first time I acknowledged the fundamental principle behind the feminine power that she represented I understood that the concept of time is an illusion we must let go of if we are to live and work freely. In that moment I realized that time is a thought form created by us. I realized that time is simply a kind of measurement applicable only to the limited form of life we live here on Earth. If you understand the now you also understand eternity. I saw that there is no difference between what has been, what is and what is to come. Everything unfolds in the moment. There is not one moment in time when what we experience as past and future is not also revealed to us in the present as a totality in eternity. Now, now, now and now! Understanding that makes it easier to understand the words attributed to Yeshua, 'Only the one who knows the beginning knows the end.'

This is the cosmic principle. It is eternity. It doesn't divide the moment into past, present and future. If it did, it wouldn't exist as anything else but memory. That's the cosmic principle. That's eternity. It doesn't divide the moment up into past, present and future. Because the future becomes the past without any chance of holding on to anything at all.

Now I see cosmic unity, or what religion calls God, everywhere! Now I *see* it!

I now understand that there is no difference between here and there. There really is no outer space. Outer space is just like the inner space. There is no difference. This realization, the way it has been shown to me, is the first step towards relinquishing gravity. Let go of the physical element, penetrate the ethereal aspect and transcend the astral and the mental aspect – unite with causality – change all that has petrified and stagnated. This is the recognition of the moment as the highest synthesis of humanity's collective experiences brought into being right NOW.

This acknowledgement is identical with total healing – because you realize that diseases are a hopeless illusion – an unnecessary crutch. When time has outplayed its role as an instrument for measurement and when human beings no longer see themselves as separate beings apart from the cosmos, the laws of karma will end.

This is dharma: bringing the sublimated moment to its full blossoming of total compassion for all living things, in harmony with what should or should not be done.

The personality, forever chasing after recognition and being something special, always looking for separation, is the laboratory where transformation occurs for every individual. When humanity, to the extent it does today, identifies itself so totally with personality's limiting strategies and templates, it cuts itself off from those qualities, which can transform imprisonment into freedom.

The sun rose behind the clouds but sent, from time to time, a single ray through a gap, drew corridors of light in the air and embraced the valley in an almost supernatural, soft morning light. I packed the tent, put everything on my back and started the descent. I carried the image of Mariam's star in my heart. Its power was so strong that I practically floated down the narrow path.

The Seer was preparing breakfast when I returned to the house in the village. He looked tired. I told him about the experiences of the night and the morning and he nodded both compassionately and happily. At the same time, however, I thought I sensed a certain amount of sorrow in his happiness. Something that moderated my own happiness which made me hold back.

I made myself a cup of instant coffee. Someone was tickling the back of my neck and it was difficult concentrating on making the coffee. Without thinking about it I said:

'Stop it Mariam!'

The Seer looked up from his cup with a surprised look on his face.

'Did you say something?'

I couldn't hold back any longer and trying to keep a straight face, laughing, I said:

'Mariam is teasing me.'

He regained his normal expression and said:

'Well, sort of clears things a bit eh?'

It felt like an angel walking through the room. In a split second all heaviness turned to light and laughter. Even the air in the small kitchen seemed to sparkle with the pollen of angels. The Seer had a big smile on his face. I laughed out loud as I hadn't laughed for many years.

He looked indulgently at me:

'How about going to the coast tomorrow? You look as if you

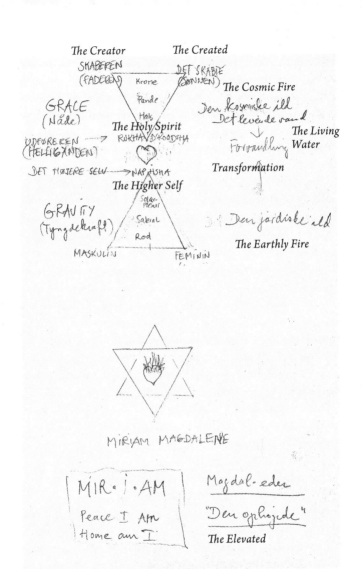

The Star of Mariam
(From the author's notebook)

could do with a change of air before you dissolve completely.'

The coast meant back to the Seer's house on the sunny coast of Andalusia. Why not? I was far too enraptured to give it a second thought. However, I did feel a strong inclination to agree with the suggestion. Perhaps I was beginning to understand the principles involved if you want to step into the flow of things.

We didn't go up into the mountains for a change. Instead, we shopped for lunch, which we took out in the open on the banks of the wide mountain stream far into the Montségur valley. It is an indescribable, peaceful spot, which has become my favourite place. You don't talk here. You *are*. No beating about the bush. No defences. Open to the higher energies.

The trickle of water in the brook was balm to my soul, which sang and danced in harmony with the beings of light around us. The light went all the way into the darkest nooks and crannies of my body, where it loosened old attitudes and set free rigid repressions, which had collected there. A coat of stubborn inertia and all my reservations dissolved and transformed into sparkling stardust rising upwards on the updraft of power from the water. I let myself dissolve in the nature of the water. A fine, ethereal blue light shone through and from it. I followed the stream and saw the blue light gather force to become a vibrating cathedral-like arch above the deepest part of the stream. A large rock rose above the surface of the water at the same spot. A faint, vibrating strip of white light cut the arch vertically to form a cross. The activity of the beings of light was more intense here and it seemed to me they were chanting an unknown hymn in the silence. Perhaps silence itself had its source in such hymns. Then I heard myself unhesitatingly saying my own Aramaic prayer: *rukha d'koodsha, malkoota d'shmeya, rukha d'koodsha, malkoota d'shmeya, rukha d'koodsha malkoota d'shmeya*, while someone was crying silently deep inside me.

The Seer sat half asleep on a bench with a smile on his face. I watched him and wondered where he came from. Which star did he belong to? But there was no answer, or maybe I just wasn't able to hear it. I thought that his smile had the same secrecy about it as Da Vinci's *Mona Lisa*. Seeing him like this I wanted most of all to kiss him on his forehead, but I didn't. I smiled inside at the thought; how he would have looked if I had. The feeling, however, was very real and I placed a kiss there anyway but on the ethereal level only.

Late in the afternoon it became cooler. I dried my eyes, packed up our things and woke the Seer. 'What happened?' he said a little dizzily putting his hand up to his forehead. He was more awake than even when he, apparently, was asleep.

Darkness and cold came creeping like two ghosts that laid their cloaks over the town and the valley. In the pale light from the few streetlights one could glimpse blue-grey smoke signals rising from the chimney stacks.

After eating a simple evening meal we lit the fire in the banqueting hall.

The Seer sat down in the only armchair in the house with his legs casually placed on a foot-stool while I sat down on a bearskin rug on the floor. Then he said:

'I have the feeling that our trip to the south is going to open yet another door to the mystery.'

'You still don't think that Saunière and the Rennes-le-Château mystery has anything to do with Mariam Magdalene?'

We were both familiar with the colourful story about the small town of Rennes-le-Château and the priest Saunière who in 1886, during major repair work on the altar of the local church, had apparently found a number of documents containing information which transformed him from a poor minister on the fringes of society to a rich man with unlimited funds and a fashionable circle of acquaintances.

Saunière had spent part of his fortune on the restoration of the church. He further built a new house, 'Bethanie', as well as a tower, 'Tour Magdala'. Saunière died in 1917 leaving the secret with his housekeeper of many years, Marie Dénarnaud, who promised to disclose it on her deathbed. Unfortunately, when that day came in 1953, she was paralysed by a stroke and was thus unable to disclose anything at all. Apparently the secret of Saunière was buried with her.

Since then, the mystery had been made the subject of many speculations, several of which had revitalized the legend of Mary Magdalene and her alleged escape from Palestine to the south of France after the death of Yeshua.

The mystery, furthermore, was linked to the story of the Templars and a secret society called the Priory of Sion which among its Grand Masters counted names such as *Nicholas Flamel (1398–1418), René d'Anjou (1418–80), Sandro Filipepi (1484–1510), Leonardo da Vinci (1510–19), Robert Fludd (1595–1637), Johann Valentin Andrea (1637–54), Robert Boyle (1654–91), Isaac Newton (1691–1727), Charles Radclyffe (1727–46), Charles of Lorraine (1746–80), Charles Nodier (1801–44), Victor Hugo (1844–85) and Jean Cocteau (1918–1963).*

We had been in Rennes on several occasions in order to visit the church and the house of Saunière, which is now a museum, and each time something touched me. The Seer, however, doubted the credibility of the mystery and had difficulty in getting in touch with what might have given us and many others certainty about the significance of the place.

The fact that Saunière went to such lengths, after finding his treasure, to camouflage his tracks in and around the church, has led people to believe that the treasure is still hidden there or somewhere in the area. But going to all that trouble might also have been a way of communicating something. Perhaps he wanted to communicate knowledge that as a minister he couldn't communicate directly because, if known, it might have gone against one or more of the church's indisputable dogmas.

'This really is a delicate matter,' the Seer replied and the drowsy look returned to his eyes.

Never before had we discussed the old legends that maintained that Mary Magdalene, immediately after the crucifixion, left the Holy Land and arrived in France, more precisely at the small coastal town of Saintes-Maries-de-la-Mer, to the west of Marseilles. One of several folk traditions states that she carried the Holy Grail with her, and that she spent the rest of her life in the caves around Sainte-Baume where she died very old. Some people feel that this Grail was the Holy Chalice used by Yeshua at the Last Supper and the one that Joseph of Arimathea used to collect the blood of Yeshua while he was still hanging on the cross. Others thought that the real secret was that *San graal* should really be read as *Sang raal*, meaning *Holy Blood* and that this blood was brought to France by Mary Magdalene in the shape of a child, the fruit of Mary's intimate relationship with Yeshua. All of this rested on a major folk tradition, the origin of which no one knew. How did such myths originate and why did they keep growing in strength, when no one could trace them back to credible sources or hard evidence?

Indisputable, however, is the fact that a large number of churches in the South of France have been named after Mary Magdalene. Furthermore, she is celebrated each year on 22 July in many places in that area. The church in Maximin even claimed that it kept the remains of St Mary Magdalene

safe and that these were the relics that were carried in a procession each year on that day, commemorating her.

Reflecting on the subject it suddenly struck me that I had read somewhere that as far back as anyone remembered, large populations of Jews had lived in Provence. Perhaps this had some connection with the arrival of Mariam? I suggested this to the Seer. He looked into the fire for a long time before answering:

'The Jews also inhabited large parts of Spain at the time. They say that Toledo, which as far as they know is the oldest town in Spain, was established around a Jewish settlement.'

'What can you say about the Jews? It looks as if they have been persecuted regularly throughout history. What kind of destiny is that?'

'That is a very good question,' he said looking into the flames. 'When I ask about the Jewish people, I am told that they are outside of everything. That they, more than any other people, come from somewhere else. It sounds cryptic but this is the answer I'm getting. It looks as if they have been appointed the guardians of something unique and a very special secret. Some of them, apparently, have misunderstood their task. Something has gone entirely wrong.'

'Where does the idea come from that they are the chosen people of God?'

'The God of Israel, the Old Testament God, has always been a limited God. Or let me put this another way: some of the Jews created their own zealous, jealous and punishing God. As time went by, this became the God to whom the Jews turned. It is a question with many facets, which makes one think. You see, it is a question of whether or not this was the same God which was adopted by Christianity and, with few modifications, made its own.'

I considered his reply, which matched my own thoughts on the subject. But what had gone wrong with the task that the Jews had been asked to manage?

I somehow sensed that this was one of the questions to which we had to find an answer if we were to solve the riddle about Mariam.

The fire had died out and we decided that it was time to go to bed.

When I was in my room I began reading a book. After half an hour it felt as though I had sand in my eyes. I woke up with a start as the book fell on to the floor. I was just about to turn the light out when I saw her. I couldn't help smiling. I knew that the picture had been there for many years. I had slept in this room many times without thinking about it. Perhaps because she had become so familiar to people, an icon used everywhere, an illustration on everything from T-shirts to matchboxes and plastic bags: *the Mona Lisa*. She smiled at me from the flowered wallpaper. I returned her smile, let go and travelled into other worlds.

8

As if by magic, Mariam's life again took another direction, a more stable one. Under the skilled tuition of Salome, day by day and slowly but surely, she was taught the deepest secrets and the way of life of the Therapists. The teaching started at sunrise and ended long after sunset. They had two meals a day consisting of roots, herbs and bread spiced with hyssop and salt.

In the beginning Mariam was taught everything about the cycles of life and the effect of the cosmos on human beings. She was taught to see her own moon cycle as a microcosmic reflection of the powers surrounding human beings.

'The moon cycle opens up many possibilities for the woman who wants to learn to look into other worlds. All the great female seers from the beginning of time have had this possibility. There are several levels on which the priestess may expand her vision. When the egg breaks away the possibilities of seeing into the astral realities increase. During the moon time itself, her ability to see into the ethereal worlds is heightened: the upper as well as the lower ones. But she must be aware of and able to sharpen the connection to the higher Self in spite of the complications offered by the moon time. If you surrender to those complications and make room for them in your mind then you will have forfeited all your options.'

Salome had brought Mariam along to the lake where they were sitting looking across the shining surface.

'When a woman lies with a man there are moments when both have the possibility of looking into other worlds, even travelling there. There are moments then, when the woman may be able to leave her body and put on her gown of stars. When you know the secrets of your body and know your mind and the possibilities and traps connected with the power of your mind, you'll be able to travel through time and space. I shall show you this when you are ready for it.'

Mariam felt a spark from a long forgotten longing in her abdomen. Salome's words reminded her of the man to whom she was engaged, but whom she did not even know and had not seen for several years. She suddenly remembered the morning when she saw him riding to her childhood home in Bethany. Although she only saw him from a distance she imagined that she remembered the features of his melancholy face. Or maybe it was an image she had created in order to have something to cling to? The engagement was the desire of her parents. Thus it was also her wish. Her parents had chosen wisely. And the strange visions she had seen of the old woman with white hair seemed to confirm this, although in these visions nothing had really been said directly about it.

Salome was watching her student and tried to read her thoughts, but she didn't say anything since she knew that it wouldn't be long before Mariam would ask about the things which occupied her mind the most, and which would come to fill her life more and more in the immediate future. Instead she said:

'When a woman is about to give birth to a child, the moment the child comes into the world she will become one with the great certainty. She will know everything. At this moment she knows the child leaving her body, knows its traits, the qualities of its soul and the sphere from which it comes. If the woman is able to go beyond the pain and other complications, the moment the head of the child appears, she will know life's deepest secrets.'

Deep within herself Mariam felt something opening up. Unknown doors squeaked on rusty hinges. She felt slightly moist between her thighs and her cheeks got warm. She turned her face away.

'Don't be shy. Set your body and your feelings free. It is only natural for a woman to sense something in the lower regions when she is confronted with words like these. This is understood by all women. It is all part of women's physical potential and the secrets we guard, more or less consciously. The danger in working with all this lies not in our immediate physical reactions like your present reaction, but in the limitation which makes us believe that our one and only unavoidable task on earth is bearing children. We must have children, and it is the task of women to bear them. But it is not woman's only and highest purpose.'

They sat for a while. Salome sensed the new kind of power awakening in her student. The afternoon was spent working in the herb garden and Salome took the opportunity to introduce a few herbs to Mariam. She pointed to a group of plants:

'Yarrow and pigeon's grass along with sage, rosemary, camomile and lady's mantle are among the oldest known women's herbs. They are used in various mixtures when a woman is in her moon time.'

'And these may be useful when a woman is going to be intimate with a man.'

She pointed to a small group of herbs in a separate herbal bed:

'This is an orchid from Galilee. You boil the root and then eat it. It is very stimulating and combined with jujube it puts a woman into a state of relaxation and openness. You may add a small amount of mandrake and nutmeg. Used properly, it may give both a man and a woman potential they never dreamed possible.'

She smiled secretively.

'But the herbs are only aids. The power itself must be manifested through your own ability to get help from the higher worlds. By way of training your willpower and the purity of your thoughts you may attract the attention of the very beings you need in a given situation. When you understand the coherence of everything, nothing can stand in your way. That is why you must learn about the endless power of praying. You must know about the real meaning of rituals and understand that they are necessary aids for you to receive the powers flowing your way through the medium of prayer. Not like the priests of Jerusalem to whom the performance of rituals for the sake of the rituals themselves is all that matters. That is why the priests are now worshipping a God made of their own limitations.'

Salome stretched herself. She had been standing bent over for too long.

'But there is a time for everything. The body must be satisfied just like the spirit. For a woman the two are inseparable. The merging of body and spirit is the realization of the perfect human being for a woman. The union of man and woman is holy and pure when it is performed in the right spirit, at the right time and with the right intentions. Do not let anyone convince you that there is anything shameful or sinful in such a union. The true union is called *certainty*. It is called this for a reason. If it wasn't holy it would never have got a name like that. Nothing created can be shameful or sinful. If the sexual act is sinful then so are the genitals. But God created them. How could God create something sinful and undignified? When the sexual act is performed in a spirit of holiness, nothing can be more holy and pure. When a man becomes one with a woman at a higher level, together they manifest the Holy Spirit. Human thought of woman is able to expand and return to its source. When she searches for her source she will be guided by the heavenly light in which she was born. She and he are one. When the two thoughts are reborn they become one ray of light. The heavenly light is drawn down by the power of thought. In this way the presence of the Eternal One is manifested on earth.'

They stopped working around noon and Salome brought Mariam to the gathering at the temple. For the first time Mariam saw the other inhabitants at close quarters. Until now, she had only seen figures dressed in white at a distance, moving about silently.

There were men and women of all ages. They all greeted each other with the word *shlama* (peace). In the temple the members sat on low benches along the curved walls, the men to the right and the women to the left. When all were present an elderly woman got up and quietly started chanting:

'Heavenly Queen
Through whom all light shines.
You light-giving Unity.
Beloved One in the highest as on earth,
You are crowned with a Tiara.
The highest of the true Priestesses.
My Lady, You are the guardian
Of the holy teaching.
In Your hand You hold the seven potentialities:
In it You hold life's innermost power,
You have gathered all the possibilities of life,
And bear them as a jewel on your breast.
We thank You for allowing us to share in Your Wealth.
Amen.'

She then turned to those gathered:

'Dear brothers and sisters. Today we have a new sister among us. Her name is Mariam. She is under the protection of sister Salome.'

She then said to Mariam:

'Greetings sister Mariam. You are most welcome.'

Everybody nodded towards Mariam. Immediately after, the woman carefully produced a note to the sound of 'aum'. A short time after they all hummed the same note and the same sound. At first the voices seemed insecure until they found the right note and suddenly all the voices became one. Mariam felt how the voices vibrated in her body. She felt that it made the whole room vibrate and somehow mysteriously connected them all in a wordless prayer. Mariam had her eyes closed and concentrated on a luminous dot in the dark. Slowly it came closer, getting bigger and bigger. The sound modulated and everything seemed to vibrate to 'mmmmmmmmmm'. The centre exploded and the note manifested itself as pulsating light:

~~~~~~
~~~~~~
~~~~~~

Slowly Mariam came back to herself. Some of the women were crying. Others stood up and chanted prayers above the note, which was subsiding. The whole room was filled with its cleansing presence. Mariam saw radiating beings dancing in the air.

The men then sang a hymn of thanks. Then the women. The meeting ended with everybody singing together.

Silently they went back to the house filled with the power that had accumulated during the gathering. It was Mariam who broke the silence:

'What happened?'

'Through our song we not only invoke forces from outside which we need at this moment. We vitalize the Holy Spirit,

Rukha d'koodsha, which is present everywhere, just waiting for us to open up and bid it welcome just as you saw it happen a while before. The Holy Spirit is not only present at the ethereal level around us, it also lives within us. Human beings are not normally conscious of their breathing. If you try not to breathe you'll find that it isn't possible. There is a power doing it for us.'

Mariam nodded. She started to see some connections. Salome continued:

'When we become aware of our breathing we take part in a collective prayer. We then unite with everything living and our Heavenly Source. Thus, the power of the Holy Spirit is revitalized in and around us. This is the first step into unity.'

They worked in the herb garden the rest of the day. At sunset they walked to the temple in order to participate in the prayers and the hymns of thanksgiving which were to manifest the Power.

Months passed like that. Mariam was a vigilant student. Step by step Salome led her into the secret halls of learning. Every day their relationship grew stronger.

Mariam woke up one morning to the sound of Salome's voice chanting a hymn that she didn't recognize. The sun had not yet risen but Mariam knew that this was going to be a special day. She got up in a hurry and went outside where Salome was sitting on a sheep's skin with a woollen blanket around her, facing east. She was surrounded by a warm radiating aura. The sight filled Mariam with an unspeakable bliss and she fell to her knees. Salome spoke to her:

'I came out of the mouth of the Highest One
and covered the earth as spirit.
I dwelt in Heaven

136

and my throne is a sacred couch.
I alone saw the Kingdom of Heaven
and recognized the deepest depth.
I have the power over the water and the earth
and over each single, living being.
He created me from the beginning, before the creation
     of the world.
I shall never fail.
I served him in the Holy of Holies.
and manifested myself in Zion.
He made me guard and rest in his beautiful town,
Jerusalem the most beautiful of roses.
I'm a river outlet.
by which I water the flowers of the garden.
I said, "I'm going to water the most important garden
and bring nourishment to the base of the roots."
And see, the brook became a river,
and the river became a sea.
Once more my doctrines will shine like the morning,
and I will send Her light into the furthest corners of
     the earth.
I will send my doctrines out like prophecies
and leave them to eternity.
All this I do not for my own sake
but for all those who seek wisdom.'

Salome stood up in front of Mariam. Salome's flames now surrounded both of them and Mariam saw that the ethereal was a thin blanket of radiating particles connected to each other. Salome drew a band of light in the air with her hand shaping it into a ball which she moved towards Mariam.

'Have no fear, but relax and open yourself to this force.'
Slowly she placed the ball of light in Mariam's lap.

'*Ephatah* – Open yourself! I now place this force into Creation (the Root Centre) where it will heal and enlighten all that has been broken and which is now in darkness.'

She then placed one of her hands on Mariam's pubic bone and the other on the lower part of her backbone.

'Be healed and blessed.'

Mariam immediately felt a lightening movement in her abdomen. Something dissolved and disappeared while a new, live power seemed to be born in her. Salome repeated the ritual at the other centres: The Power (the sacral centre), the Self (solar plexus), Love (the heart), the Will (the throat), clarity (the Forehead), and Neshemah (the crown – the bridge to the higher Self). She repeated the words, 'Be healed and blessed' seven times and drew a cross with arms of equal length in front of each of the centres. The air was alive with active powers. Salome ended the simple initiation ritual.

'Give me your hand.'

Mariam stretched her hand out towards Salome.

'Hold it steady and concentrate on the subtle pulse in your fingertips. At the same time, from your Heavenly Consciousness draw down balanced light through your crown and radiate the light of prophecy from your throat centre, letting the two unite in your brow, sending that light through to your fingertips. Now sense the even finer transition between the skin and the air. Feel, how, with your outermost pulse, you are able to touch the pulse of the ethereal.'

An intense energy flowed through Mariam. It was like putting your hand into a beehive, the only difference being that this power was painless. It was an enlightened state.

'Now, dissolve the thin barrier between the fingers and the air. The two elements are one and the same. You surrender the pulse of your fingers to that of the ethereal. You give up any kind of resistance without getting too eager.'

In a short flash Mariam sensed a kind of fusion. But then she lost it all and had to start all over again. Salome drew a radiating circle in the air with great patience, in order to demonstrate the basic principle.

'You might say that paradoxically this is the only kind of physical contact with Heaven you may practise with. Because the principle is the same, be it lower or higher. The secret is about being obliging without being obtrusive. We so quickly reach the limitations of our concepts when we try to express this. But if for a while you are able to give up all of your own pettiness and surrender in total confidence, and at the same time you are fully concentrated, then you will succeed.'

Salome drew light onto Mariam's fingertips. Just before their fingers met, Mariam had the same feeling as when you burst a soap bubble with your finger. At that moment a hole appeared in the bubble and Mariam sensed a connection between them, a spark flew and a mild vibration extended to her knuckles. Salome pulled her hand away. Mariam then to her great surprise saw how the light followed the hesitant movements of her own fingers, leaving a thin, uneven line in the air.

'This isn't something that you may impress people with, since only very few people will be able to see it. Most people, however, will be able to feel it. Especially when you start healing people.'

Mariam kept on drawing with her finger in a hectic attempt to maintain the light which, however, kept getting weaker and weaker until it disappeared completely.

'You now understand the principle. The rest is a matter of practice.'

Salome let go of her seriousness and welcomed the breaking of dawn with her tinkling laughter.

'This is how you open up to the powers of healing. Surrender to *Rukha d'koodsha*. Through practice and prayer you will finally become so good at uniting with the Holy Spirit that it will participate in everything you do. Everything that you think, everything you do will be an extension of this prayer. Everything you touch will turn into light. All your actions will have a healing effect.'

After half a year during which Salome continued teaching Mariam the noble art of healing, she realized, that not only did Mariam live up to all her expectations, but, furthermore, this woman was made from a rare, radiating matter. Once in a while, however, Mariam disappeared into a state of sadness and melancholy. But Salome saw her and understood that these phases were inevitable. She remembered her own struggles on her innermost levels when she herself was being educated.

The battle between heaven and earth continued until the day she finally realized there was no difference between them; that they were simply reflecting poles of equal strength. Now she experienced it all once more through Mariam.

'Sorrows and wants aren't just something we have to go through. Sorrows and wants also have to go through us, so to speak,' she said one day when Mariam seemed more sad than usual.

'Thoughts travel through the cosmos. Once in a while they pass through us. Not in order to destroy us but in order to be transformed. We just shouldn't identify with the chaos arising during this change. The conditions are secondary. Only the transformation itself has any value. The time is getting close when you'll understand.'

Salome made a few exaggerated, melancholy gestures. Slowly she began circling around Mariam while she made the saddest face she could muster. It didn't take long before the medicine worked and shortly after they were both dancing around in the courtyard laughing, with the goats watching them in astonishment.

After a year, the day Salome had been waiting for arrived.

She woke Mariam up long before sunrise and asked her to get ready for departure. The sudden change in the normally set routine surprised Mariam and she was besieged by her old worries.

'Don't be afraid,' Salome said soothingly, 'this is probably the most beautiful part of your education.'

They prepared the donkeys, tied two big water jars onto them and set out. Mariam soon realized that they were on their way into the wilderness. She wondered about Salome's sudden haste. When they had been riding for a couple of hours Salome turned away from the caravan track, between some rocks and along a mountain path. Halfway up the mountain they had to get off and lead the animals. They stopped on a ledge in front of a cave. Salome started unloading the water jars. She pointed to the cave and said to Mariam:

'This will be your home for the next forty days. When you have used the water, you may fill the jars at the brook higher up on the mountain. It will not be difficult for you. This is the final and decisive test. If you pass this one you'll know everything that I cannot tell you in words anyway. This cleansing is a prerequisite for true vision. It will sharpen your natural ability to see. You'll find a natural beehive in the cave. Here you'll be able to find your sustenance. Be prepared. Do not let yourself be swept away by melancholy and self-pity. Whatever happens, do not let yourself be tempted by anyone or anything. Concentrate on the practices and the prayers that I taught you. Remember

141

where you come from, what you are made of, and where you are going. Stay courageous. I shall come and get you when the forty days are over.'

She embraced Mariam, kissed her on her forehead and gave her one of the holy scrolls of the Therapists. Mariam took Salome's hand and held it to her lips.

'I shall not let you down.'

She stayed on the ledge and watched Salome ride back until both rider and donkey disappeared and became a dot on the horizon.

The first few days in the cave were spent getting used to the new surroundings. Without any disturbances other than the wind, the wild animals and the delusions of the mind, Mariam slowly came closer to a nearness, a new kind of awareness, that saw everything as one, freed from sentimentality, clear-cut.

On the seventh day she was like an open wound. The daylight blinded her and the realities of life played out relentlessly in the sand in front of her right where she sat watching ants working hard carrying food to the anthill.

Everything was painfully clear.

She suddenly sensed another presence.

'I am Metatron, the angel of the Covenant. This is the Kingdom and the Restraint. This is the harmony towards the end and thus the harmony of a new beginning. Adonai, Adonai, I prostrate myself before you. You the queen, Shekhinah – Eve, the first woman. On this day you acknowledge the instincts – on this your own day, you transform them. The path of self-discipline awaits you. Here you are going to regain your true self-respect. Make peace with life's inevitable loneliness. Accept your destiny, bidding you to walk in confidence.'

The very being of the angel quietly united with Mariam. Then it disappeared as suddenly as it had appeared.

Mariam spoke the first line of her favourite prayer:
'Heavenly Source.'

Suddenly she understood that this Source was a Power where both poles are present. It was both father and mother and yet not either of them. And she saw clearly that the fact that only the masculine form was used didn't mean that you celebrated one of the poles only. She suddenly saw that in reality there was only one sex and that the masculine and the feminine were simply the extremities of this one sex.

On the twelfth day Mariam spoke the second line: *'You who are everywhere.'* She saw that everything is suffused with the Holy Spirit, the possibility for the manifestation of life. She saw that this was the Foundation and that everything returns to the place of origin. Here the sun rose. Here it set.

On the thirteenth day she confirmed her knowledge with the words: *'Hallowed be Thy name.'*

And she saw the clarity and the greatness of what had been created. She understood that everything was vitalized through the name. Everything was born through the power of acknowledgement.

When eighteen days had passed she spoke the words: *'Thy Kingdom come.'*

With these words she made the highest wish of her prayer come true. This was victory over the self wanting to decide its own path. You must walk the path of death and of rebirth. This is the great transformation.

On the twentieth day she placed the following words in her heart: *'Thy will be done, here and now and in eternity.'*

This was the true source of leniency and beauty. This was the birthplace of life and death, the active morals and ethics of this world. *Rukha d'koodsha, malkoota d'shmeya.*

After twenty-one days she prayed: *'Fill us with the power of Thy grace.'*

143

With these words she understood that mankind was not always given what it wanted, but always received what it needed. Thus, she knew that this was the golden road of justice. Here your destiny was decided by what you yourself placed on the scales.

It demanded strength to surrender to this path. Grace, love and compassion were waiting at its end.

On the twenty-second day of Mariam's fast: *'And set us free from the chains with which we bind ourselves and each other.'*

Move everything which is locked. Free me from every lie, all my reservations and every judgement with which I chain my brothers and sisters and myself. Help me to look on them with the same leniency with which I want them to look on me.

On the twenty-fourth day she whispered: *'Lead us out of temptation: Free us from ourselves.'*

Help me not to let my egoistical mind limit my understanding of this life. Pull the veils aside and let me see the truth as it is. Only then do I understand my real Self and Your Kingdom where all living things share Your Holy Spirit. Lead me along the path of Love, the true path of my emotions.

On that day for the first and only time she read in the scroll that Salome had given her. Here she found the words of the divine Hermes:

'The incorporeal cannot be embraced by anything. But it may itself embrace everything. It is the fastest of all things – and the greatest. Think about your real Self and you'll know that it is so.

'Bid your soul to travel to any country you may choose, and faster than you may bid it go, it will arrive there.

'Bid it go from land to sea and no less quickly will it be there. It does not move as you move from one place to another, it simply is there.

'Bid it fly to the sky and it shall not need wings. Nothing can bar its way, neither the extreme heat of the sun nor the whirling motion of the planet spheres. Moving through everything it will fly upwards to the outermost limits of all bodily things. And should your wish be to break away from the universe itself in order to look at things from the external side of the cosmos, then even that will be possible. Imagine the power, imagine the speed you possess. And when you yourself can do this, cannot the Power do the same? Thus, you must understand that this is the way that the Power contains all of the cosmos, itself and everything that is. It is like the thoughts that the Power is thinking, the fact that everything is contained within it.

'If therefore you do not compare yourself to the Power, you will not be able to understand it. For like recognizes like.

'Rise above all that is of the body and let yourself grow to a size equal to the greatness which is beyond all measure.

'Rise above all of time and become eternal, then you shall understand the Power.

'Think that, for you also, nothing is impossible.

'Consider that you are also immortal and that you are able to understand all things in your mind, and that you are able to understand any kind of art and any kind of science.

'Find your home in the abode of any living creature.

'Rise above any height and go down below any depth.

'Unite within yourself the opposites of all qualities, warm and cold, dry and moist. Imagine that you are everywhere at the same time, on land, at sea and in the sky.

'Imagine that you have not yet been born, that you are still in the womb, that you are old, that you are dead, that you are in the world beyond the grave.

'Keep all this in your mind at the same time, all time and all places, all substances and potentials in one. Then you may understand the Power. However, if you lock your soul in your body and demean yourself and say, "I know nothing, I can do nothing, I'm afraid of the earth and the sea and I cannot rise to the sky. I do not know what I was, and not what I'm going to be." If you say this, what connection can you have with the Power?

'Your mind cannot understand any of that which is beautiful and good if you cling to the body and do not know anything about the higher levels. The peak of ignorance is not knowing the Power. But the ability to know the Power and wanting and hoping to be able to know it, is the path that leads to the higher consciousness. And it is an easy path. The Power will meet you everywhere, it will appear everywhere, at any time and any place, in your waking hours and during your sleep, travelling across the sea and any water, at night and during the day, when you speak and when you are silent. There is nowhere and nothing in which the Power is not present.'

On the twenty-eighth day she surrendered silently: *'And lend us the power to be one with You.'*

When she spoke these words she saw that they were an expression of Wisdom, the prime thought of the Father now wanting to unite with its divine source.

Opening her eyes she now saw that she was no longer in her body but hovering above the mountain. Below her she saw a young woman squatting in prayer on the ledge. And she understood the words once said by Salome: As above, let it be below.

Floating about in her star body she let herself be surged by SHM, the heavenly semen and became pregnant with Wisdom. Above her she noticed an unknown force called *Kether*. Its open eye scanned everything. A little later the eye

146

closed and the force changed its identity to *Ein Sof.* At the same moment the universe stopped existing. Only when the being once again opened its eye did this Nothingness cease.

At that moment Mariam realized that the other half of that being, *Eva, Shekhinah, Hokhmah, Barbelo, Ishtar, Isis, Sophia,* was slowly beginning to bud and grow within her. Throughout the universe there was only one sound:

Amen.

When after forty days Salome came to collect her student she became worried when she did not find anything but an empty cave and Mariam's white blanket. She looked further into the cave, but Mariam was nowhere to be seen. A sudden impulse made her climb higher up the mountain. Getting to the summit she was met by a sight, which she might have dreamt about, but which she had not dared hope she could ever really come to see. On the edge of the cliff sat Mariam surrounded by an unspeakably intense and beautiful light which made Salome fall to her knees with her face turned away. But that which made her heart swell with emotion was the sight of Mariam floating in the air about twenty centimetres above the ground, fervently in silent prayer.

Above them could be heard a voice:

'This is my daughter, Mariam, in whom I am well pleased. Today she has received the name Magdalene, the Exalted Spirit of Peace. I have come back to the world in her shape. By her power shall humanity understand its destiny. Through her shall humanity again find peace.'

9

Mona Lisa was still smiling when I woke up.

Coming back to my everyday consciousness I was struck by the thought that maybe she was Leonardo da Vinci's secret formula for the isogynic being. An image of the condition in which an individual, irrespective of sex, both integrates and dissolves the masculine and the feminine within, so that he or she is both one and the other and yet neither of them. Behind this the most famous smile in the world was not only a woman but also a man, perhaps the creator of the painting, Da Vinci himself. Was it Da Vinci's own eyes that looked so teasingly at me from the wall at the foot of my bed?

My nocturnal journey had taken me to the astral reality. I roamed numerous spheres where I was confronted with various repressions and prejudices, all of which led back to episodes in my life, no matter how strange they might seem.

In short periods of time, however, I did move more freely, getting help to change some of the burden I was carrying, and it was very liberating to see dark matter change into light. The mornings when I returned from such travels I was very tired on waking up, though I was filled with energy when I first got up.

That morning I used the energy to clean the house and pack my suitcase.

A couple of hours later the Seer and I were on our way south. We crossed the Pyrenees at Andorra and continued towards Saragossa. As we drove into Spain it became clear that a new page had turned in the old manuscript, which the Seer had placed in my care a few years earlier. It wasn't just a mental experience but an actual, physical one, causing the well-known phenomenon synchronicity when, for example, two people say exactly the same thing at exactly the same time:

'Did you feel that?' we asked simultaneously, our eyes meeting in wonder.

Something was going on.

In front of us the road cut straight as a die through a flat and bare landscape. I was considering the thoughts we had discussed the previous day about the strange fate of the Jews and not least their settlements in the south of France and Spain which could be traced back to the time before Christ. Something told me that the mystery in which we were participating was somehow connected to this people and their powerful religious background.

Because of my Aramaic studies, a language closely connected with and a prerequisite for understanding Hebrew, I knew something about Jewish mysticism, the basis of the Kabbalah. I also knew the numerical value of each of the signs and the qualities that each one represented.

The Kabbalah, which means 'that which has been transmitted', is connected with a special historical Jewish movement that arose in Provence in the south of France during the first half of the 12th century. I was now wondering about the fact that, quite strangely, this coincided with the year 1180 when a Jewish Sufi master, Kyot from Toledo, is said to have brought a secret manuscript from his home town in Spain to Provence, which described the secret of the Grail. Nevertheless, it is here, for the first time, we meet the expression the 'Holy Grail'. Could it be possible that this Grail was connected to the Kabbalah? On confronting the Seer with these thoughts, he responded:

'Why don't we stop in Kyot's hometown, Toledo? It is situated a little to the south of Madrid. It'll be no problem – not much of a detour. Maybe we'll find something out.'

We got to Toledo late in the afternoon. The old part of the city is situated on a ridge and surrounded by the River Tajo and it has a kind of cool, aristocratic reticence. Its history reaches far back into the unknown, and no one really knows about its origin. One legend tells us that it was built around a Jewish settlement, but no one knows the exact year. Other sources claim that it was built by the Romans.

We drove through Puerta del Sol and followed the small streets to the Alcázar Palace where we parked the car. We found a small hotel in a side street, the Imperial, and decided to spend the night there. It was the obvious thing to do.

At the reception desk a dark haired woman was preparing a bill for guests leaving the hotel. I looked at her while we waited. Something about her seemed familiar but I couldn't see what it was. I had never met her before. Maybe it was just one of those things which happen when a man looks at a woman and is fascinated by her. But this was different.

Then it was our turn.

She wasn't beautiful in the normal sense, but she had a personality that somehow caught your attention. She had a pair of burning eyes and moon-coloured skin. There was a kind of electric aura about her, which either attracted or repulsed you.

The Seer and I checked in, each with our own room. A little later we went out into the city to find a place to eat.

You cannot take many steps in Toledo without practically losing your way. The small streets are so narrow and the houses so relatively tall that it is difficult for the light to filter down. You step suddenly into a plaza only to be caught a little while later in a maze of blind alleys and winding passages filled with secret entrances and hidden doors.

It was in this city that the painter El Greco gained his reputation in the 16th century. It was the capital of Spain at the time, a world-famous centre for the production of swords, chain-mail armour and other weapons conjured up in the smithies, as well as being a melting pot of religions such as Christian monastic orders, Arabian Sufis, Jewish kabbalists and various alchemists living harmoniously beside merchants, dukes, princes and kings. Toledo was the centre of commerce where money flowed like honey in beehives. The city had been very rich. Now, however, it seemed more closed, perhaps as a protest against its shameful destiny of being reduced to a simple tourist trap. Or perhaps it was guarding its secrets?

'Let's have a drink' the Seer said.

We found a bar close to a small square below the hotel, and were about to enter when I noticed a sign on the wall of a house carrying the name of the square:

Plaza de la Magdalena.

It almost felt like a subtle joke, just like the Mona Lisa

reproduction with her teasing smile. Dumbfounded I pointed to it. Now the Seer also noticed.

'Someone is trying to tell us something,' he said and smiled laconically.

At the bar we both had a sandwich and a Fernet.

'It is a strangely closed city,' the Seer said, 'it seems as if it is hiding something. When I go into the universes and ask, I do not get an answer as such. However, there are other ways. Perhaps we should just sleep on it and see what happens.'

We finished our drinks and went back to the hotel. The young woman at reception had been relieved by an elderly woman whom I took to be her grandmother.

We each went to our own room.

Once in my room I lay down on my bed hoping that something would happen. I was determined to get in contact with this old master Kyot. What was it he had found in Toledo that had started the whole adventure of the Holy Grail?

I don't know how long I meditated but I must have fallen asleep, because I was suddenly on my way into the astral spheres the way I had been doing every night since the experience at the Hôtel Costes at Montségur. As usual, I floated about in a room without any visible walls. However, I had no doubt that this was a different place from the one I usually frequented, which was normally about collective and personal traumas I needed to let go of. I was now in a sphere where the sense of time was intense. It wasn't usually like this. Using a kind of projector I sent a cone of light into a narrow, dark room with characteristic, medieval stone walls. An old man with a white beard was sitting on a chair and I had no doubt at all that this was Kyot. Apparently he was in a hurry; at least this was the feeling I got since he immediately started talking:

'The Kabbalah is here in Toledo. But only the shrewdest of people will be able to find it.'

'Where?' I asked quickly.

'In the streets and passages.'

'Do the Kabbalah and the Grail have anything to do with each other?'

'Yes!'

'At the time, where did you get your knowledge from?'

'From the magus Léon from Toledo.'

'Do you know where he got it from?'

'From an itinerant magician by the name of Flegetanis, the one who talks with the stars.'

'Can it be traced back further?'

'At the beginning of time it was given to Abraham by *Melchizedek*.'

'Can you tell me anything about *Melchizedek*?'

Either Kyot didn't want to answer the last question or he didn't have the time to do it since the cone of light suddenly and without warning went out and I floated on through space to a sphere outside of time. Suddenly I was in the basement where I had been before.

At the end of a long passage a door is waiting to be opened. I walk towards it. Behind the door I expect to find the carcass of a pig, the heart of which is kept alive artificially by a machine. I open the door, but to my great surprise I find that the metal table with the pig has gone. In the middle of the room, which is no longer an operating theatre, a cream-coloured couch takes up the space instead. At one end of it a young woman is sitting, and I notice that it is the young woman from the reception desk at the Imperial Hotel.

'Welcome,' she says and motions me to sit down.

I sit down at the other end of the sofa. Now I also notice the peacefulness of the room. The pleasant atmosphere makes me relax and I feel that my thoughts are slowing down.

'I'm your oracle,' the woman states and smiles at me as if her statement is the most natural thing in the world.

'In the future you may come here and ask your questions. I cannot promise you that you'll get the answers you want or expect, but I promise you that you'll always get the answers you need in their most appropriate form.'

She looks at me intensely and I understand that this is the voice I have been hearing for the last few days, and I also understand that I shall always be able to trust this being and that she will always help me, no matter what. I have an uncontrollable urge to hold her. We are siblings, I'm in no doubt of that, but I ask her anyway:

'Who are you?'

'I am the one who has always been with you. You have called me by various names but you have avoided me too often, or you might not have been able to hear me when I tried to get through to you. Too often you have been busy

Miriam of Toledo

with your own affairs. But mark my words: this is going to change. Seek me here in this room, whenever you need me. You are always welcome, even at times when you do not have anything to ask. There may still be some answers for you.'

The room faded away and I opened my eyes. It was just after midnight. I was lying on my hotel bed not sleepy at all. Most of all I wanted a cup of coffee. Why not? I made up my mind and went down to the reception desk.

The young woman had once more taken her position behind the curved desk. Apparently she was busy doing the books and the cash register. A hidden lamp behind the counter was the only light, which made the cubicle look like a small island floating about in the empty, dark room. I let the door hit the wall on purpose in order not to frighten her with my unexpected appearance. She looked up and smiled when she saw me.

'May I help you,' she said in her charming accent.

'I'm very sorry, but I'm really in need of a cup of coffee, and I thought . . .'

'Certainly.'

She was already getting out of her seat.

'Come this way.'

I followed her into the next room where most of the tables had already been set for breakfast. A percolator was twinkling with a red light behind a small counter. I ordered a cappuccino and she asked me to sit down at one of the tables. I was watching the back of her neck and her back while she made the coffee with supple movements. It was a strange situation. I felt that I knew her and that I had always known her. It wasn't more than fifteen minutes ago that I had met her in another reality and we had spoken with each other. Now, I felt totally estranged.

She prepared the white foam on top of the coffee and

decorated it with chocolate sprinkle. A little later she balanced the cup through the air and placed it in front of me. Then she started wiping the counter and setting the last tables. I just sat and sipped my coffee in order not to finish too fast.

'By the way . . .'

She took a map of the city from the counter and turned towards me.

'Did I tell you that there are a few places that you and your friend ought to visit while you are here?'

Taken by surprise I shook my head. It seemed like a strange thing to say, given the time. She unfolded the map and let her eyes roam the heart-shaped maze. She conjured up a ballpoint pen from her breast pocket and drew a few circles on the map. She folded the map again, gave it to me and was about to turn around when I plucked up courage enough to ask her:

'Excuse me, but what is your name?'

There was a short pause and she gave me a surprised look. Then she said:

'Miriam.'

She remained standing for a while. I got up slightly confused and heard myself saying:

'My name is Lars.'

The whole situation must have seemed ludicrous.

'I know,' she said laughing.

She stayed there looking at me when I said good-night and walked back towards the staircase. It felt as if she could see straight through me.

'Good-night,' she said as the door closed behind me.

For a change, I woke up the next morning without being able to remember anything about the astral travels I had been on during the night. It was a relief. But I had the encounter

156

with Miriam quite clear in my head. Before going down for breakfast with the Seer I remembered the map that Miriam had given to me.

Sitting opposite the Seer I wanted to tell him about the experiences of the night, but something held me back.

'So, did you sleep well?'

It was the Seer's usual brisk way of greeting me, originating from his days as a senior officer in the army.

I nodded.

'I think that maybe I have found an opening.'

'Hmm, what do you mean?'

I hesitated, but then it came to me just like that. Suddenly I understood what it was Kyot had meant when he told me that the Kabbalah was in Toledo. Suddenly I realized that his cryptic answer, that the Kabbalah was to be found in the 'streets and passages', was to be taken quite literally.

'What do you think about the idea that the original town may have been built around the Tree of Life. What if the Kabbalah is shown in the original ground-plan of the town?'

'Bingo,' he said, 'I really think you've got something there. We'll start right after breakfast.'

I placed Miriam's map of the city in front of him:

'Maybe we can use this as a starting point?'

The Seer went into action an hour later. He was in high spirits and it was a pleasure to see him working. He was a study of concentration. He was in his element.

We walked through the narrow streets studying Miriam's map. We went further and further into the old Jewish quarter. The Seer suddenly stopped. The surroundings changed within seconds. A strange glow fell over the small square. It was obvious that the Seer was on his way into another universe. Then he said:

'I am in touch with Léon the Magus.'

This piece of information ought not to have surprised me with the Seer's other achievements taken into consideration, but he surprised me once more with his precision. There was no doubt in my mind that this Léon the Magus was exactly the same as the Léon of Toledo whom Kyot had talked about the previous night. The Seer continued:

'He confirms your idea that the Kabbalah was the basic model for the original town. Unfortunately, it looks as if the town has undergone so many changes since then that it is impossible to find that model. He tells me that he will point out the places but that in planning the town they worked with seven Kabbalah points only. The uppermost three and the tenth were hidden.'

He started walking while he mumbled:

'This looks promising.'

Turning a corner he stopped again. We were standing outside the Taller del Moro in the street bearing the same name. He was in his own world for a while.

'This was once the place of '*the Knowledge about that which was*'. This is the eighth centre of the present Kabbalah – '*Hod*', the Radiance. We are talking about a number of storage-kingdoms holding the consciousness of the days of yore. It is also the sphere of the Brotherhood. More cannot be said at this time.'

We hastily moved north and passed the present Universidad de San Pedro Mártir. The Seer stopped at Plaza de San Román. It was a small square with a typical Spanish statue depicting one of the forefathers of the city. There were a few cypresses on the plaza surrounded by a low hedge.

'This is the place for "*the Understanding of Alchemy*". It is the same as the fifth centre of the present Kabbalah, "*Gevurah*", Strength. Here once was situated a copy of the place outside the universe where the original knowledge about alchemy was stored. The area has an understanding of all the elements. If you are standing in the middle of the shape of a ball that is where the process is happening. In order to understand the alchemy of the elements you may use the name "Alkymium". Léon is showing me a special point relating to matter. When I ask about a sign for this place I'm given a key, which changes into an *"Ankh"*, the Egyptian Key of Life.'

I was busy writing everything he said into my notebook. It was obvious that the Seer was in contact with something very important. The diligence with which he worked was impressive. And as usual when he was in this mood, everything came quickly and precisely. I partly walked and partly trotted in order to keep up with him and tried to take notes at the same time. We went in a north-easterly direction until we got to Calle de los Carmelitas. This was also one of the places that Miriam had circled.

'This is the place for "*the Understanding of other universes*". This is the old home of the elements. This place is equivalent to the invisible centre of the Eternal Kabbalah. This centre is called *"Nut"* and has something to do with snake forms. A series of unclear patterns are showing themselves as pentagons and octagons. Léon is pointing out that they contain deep knowledge. I see a dark tunnel with widespread points of light. It is possible to break the pattern and to get out of the tunnel. Then you meet yourself as the Oracle.'

I almost fell over backwards hearing the last sentence. The Seer poured out information in a constant flow, and it was difficult to understand its cryptic content. However, the sentence about the Oracle was a confirmation of the fact, that, notwithstanding the Seer's own understanding of the information, when it appeared, it was very precise.

From the Carmelite Monastery the Seer turned south. He stopped where Calle de Santa Justa, Calle de Sal, Calle del Hombre de Palo and Calle de Cordonerías met in a small junction.

'This is the place for "*the Knowledge of the Physical*". This is equivalent to the fourth centre of the Kabbalah, "*Hesed*". Love. The image showed a symphonic body. Somewhere in the human brain there is a symphonic chamber. A symbol made from two entwined strings. Each string is made from twelve units. This symbol may be used in the physical world where harmony is missing.'

Immediately the Seer was on his way again. We passed the Catedral Primada de Toledo and walked down Calle Carcel del Vicario. Approximately halfway down the street he turned into a narrow passage.

'The next spot is right here. This is the place for "*the Human Image of Transformation*". It is equivalent to the seventh centre of the Kabbalah, "*Netzah*", Victory. It tells you about the human power of imagination, which, if used properly, may serve mankind in a positive way. By the use of this power we decide for ourselves how we want to be. Through this, we may change our shadowy part and conquer our base nature.'

We now travelled toward the south-west. The Seer sped up even more as if there was no time to be wasted. We walked briskly down Calle de Santa Isabel and stopped at a small square, which also bore this name.

'This is the place for "*Understanding the Universe*". It is equivalent to the ninth centre of the present Kabbalah – "*Yesod*", the Foundation Stone. Léon explains that in order to understand the universe you must look at it from the outside.'

The Seer slipped away again, but a little later he came back.

'The universe dances in its own quiet way. It is surrounded by fine ring-shaped auras. This thought form was once reflected in microcosm, to be more exact, here on this street. Long ago there was a brothel here. Not in the way we understand a brothel, but truly a house of pleasure, a kind of university if you like, where female dancers made the universe dance.'

He had hardly finished the last sentence before he was on the move again, now due north.

'We are on our way into the centre of the system.'

Suddenly he seemed to be more alert, more on the lookout. At the Plaza del Consistorio in front of the Ayuntamiento he circled around but didn't seem to be satisfied. Slowly, we walked into Calle de la Trinidad and followed the walls to the Palacio Arzobispal. He stopped at a side entrance and stayed there caught up in his own thoughts.

'Here it is,' he said finally. 'This is "*the Melting pot*" with the Grail in the middle. In the known Kabbalah it must be the equivalent of the sixth centre, "*Tifferet*" – the innermost Compassion. Until now, Léon has been present but I haven't been able to see Kyot. Léon is leaving us now. He says that this is the revealed town. Kyot is showing me a garden maze. He is drawing various patterns, among others the Star of David, which, really is *The Shield of Solomon*. He is showing me the 144 or twelve by twelve consciousnesses, which are the essences of each other. No matter where you are in this maze you must be able to find the Grail.'

The Seer was now looking directly at me.

'You said so yourself: "*the Grail is a state of mind*". Kyot is explaining that it was his task to be the one who removed the veil and revealed this knowledge. The legend of the Grail was and still is important to inspire mankind on its way towards self-knowledge and a higher consciousness.'

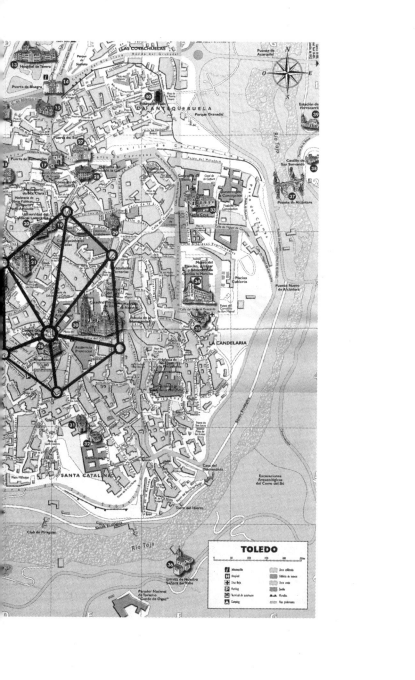

He looked wonderfully satisfied.

'That's that then,' he said with his old, sly smile.

The work of the day had been done.

From Toledo we drove towards the southern, sunny coast of Spain where we examined the impressions we had received. It was clear that a change had taken place between us. The teacher–student relationship was undergoing a change toward a more equal kind of co-operation. Especially after I had met the Oracle.

The Seer and I were two very different personalities with very different temperaments and yet I could see how, in some central areas, we were very much alike. For example we both had very strong willpower, which tended to maintain our relationship within a set framework. This was seen very clearly in our different modes of work when the results were not immediately compatible. But it was really more a matter of the interpretation and application of terms than it was a matter of the deeper meaning of those terms. We simply used our language differently.

The Seer saw me to the train as he had done so many times before.

'It is time to start your task,' he said.

When I went to wave goodbye to him from the compartment, he had already gone.

When I got back to Denmark a whole new world opened up for me. My 'new task' turned out to be working as a therapist. What kind of therapist had not been disclosed to me. It was all my own decision.

Through the abilities I had gained during my time with the Seer, I began the most instructive kind of work I had ever had, working with other people.

Each new client made me see new, unknown sides to myself. Meeting other people like that taught me that not only are we all in the same boat, but we are also brothers and sisters on the same spiritual level. We are all one big family, notwithstanding our social, political, religious or sexual affiliations. I have learned that we are made from the same matter, come from the same place and are going to the same place, though not necessarily by the same paths. We are the same and only the physical conditions differ. This task was not only filled with meaning, it was very revelatory.

I was still travelling in the astral spheres every night. Most of the time I travelled freely, but far too often I was forced to stay in the lower regions. Strangely enough, these nightly journeys had the side effect of leaving me with almost supernatural energy during the day. At one time it became such a burden that I had to seek advice from my good friend, the theosophist Søren Hauge, whom I trusted and whom I knew was familiar with the phenomenon.

It was a relief to hear him say that he knew about others with similar experiences, and that the frequency of such experiences would, in all probability, diminish in the course of time. It was a matter of becoming conscious of the spheres in which you travelled so that the traveller little by little became so adept that he himself could decide when and where he wanted to travel. Furthermore, Søren told me that it was possible to meet other astral pilgrims at the various levels, and that he knew it was possible to communicate directly with other travellers at such encounters.

Encouraged by Søren's advice, I started practising becoming goal-oriented before falling asleep. I realized that it was a matter of concentrating my thoughts on certain events in my life that I wanted to understand or get in contact with. My nocturnal journey would then probably take me to the astral copy of these events.

At other times I could return to a specific level by concentrating on a distinctive mark or a feeling that I had met at an earlier encounter here. I tried to return to the room with the cream-coloured leather couch and my oracle Miriam for a long time, but without any success.

It was during a consultation one day that I heard the Voice – Miriam – giving a piece of no-nonsense advice to a client with whom I was talking. This created a long pause and an embarrassing silence, and I must have looked rather strange while I tried to listen to this voice which, apparently, I was the only one who could hear. My client seemed quite lost when in a very kind way she tried to get in contact with me again. Luckily she was very understanding when I told her what had happened, especially when I gave her the message I had just received. It was a very precise answer to her present problem.

This event was the beginning of a whole series of similar events giving me the opportunity to develop acceptable abilities to be present and focused, while at the same time I was in contact with the Oracle. Since then, I have learned to listen to my very first intuition, which nearly always turns out to be right.

All in all I learned that a successful healing is not so much dependent on the personal ability of the healer, but more to do with the extent to which he is able to make himself a pure instrument for the Power. The first and foremost task of such an instrument is to get into a state of mind, through various practices, rituals or prayers, where the ever-present potential in and around a person is activated, so that the ethereal life force becomes a noticeable reality. In such a state you must give up any kind of judgement and prejudice. This state is very much similar to the one used by the old Taoists when describing *'the true human being'*. The true human being breathes with his whole body, arrives here almost unnoticed, is present in a quiet way of being and leaves the world silently when he has fulfilled his purpose. The healer invokes and transmits the Power without considering his own role or making a great to-do about it. Nothing else can make you feel more humble and deeply grateful than witnessing the successful outcome of such a process.

Almost two years went by like this, interrupted only by travels to Montségur and Andalusia every six months in order to meet with the Seer. During that time I constantly tried to get in contact with Miriam in the room with the cream-coloured couch but without success. But one day the phone rang . . .

10

Mariam was in her twenty-fourth year, and as an initiated priestess in the society of the Therapists had earned the right to live in her own house. She was a full member of the society and held an elevated position within the Temple as a beloved preacher and interpreter of the Scriptures. She was a magnificent healer and was visited by all kinds of diseased people who came from afar to be treated by this charismatic woman.

It was in the month of Elul, Mariam had just finished a gathering in the Temple and was on her way to her small cabin on the shores of Mareotis when she spotted Salome walking towards her in a state of agitation. Mariam immediately sensed that something out of the ordinary had happened. She knew that it would take something very special to make Salome lose her composure. The two women embraced.

'What happened?' Mariam asked her.

'Your time has come.'

Mariam felt a pang in her heart. Although she knew very well what they meant, time had slowly but surely buried deep in her memory all thought about the consequences of these words.

'When?'

'Now. The messenger from the Brotherhood is waiting for you in my house.'

Mariam was struck by fear for a brief moment, but she quickly collected herself. Salome, who knew her like a mother knows her own daughter, knew that no amount of fear could ever force Mariam away from the path she had to follow.

The Brotherhood had sent a young novice, Lamu. He handed Mariam a scroll. Mariam was again her usual self and broke the seal with a steady hand. The words from the first book of the Torah worked like a key on Mariam's heart: '*The silver cup must be found within the tribe of Benjamin.*'

The sentence almost floated out of the fresh papyrus. The key slipped unhindered into the lock. The door sprang open and she knew that the time was ripe when she had to redeem the pact her parents had made on her behalf a long time ago.

'I shall leave this very day,' she said.

Salome opened a cupboard in which she kept her most precious herbs. She handed Mariam a small alabaster jar.

'Take these 500 shekels of myrrh. You must find the remaining ingredients when you need them. Go in peace.'

She took a ring from a small pocket in her gown and placed it on Mariam's finger. It fitted her perfectly. A dark blue sapphire was placed on each side of the word '*Ephatah*', which was engraved on the ring. '*Rukha d'koodsha*' was engraved on the reverse side of the ring.

'Put it on when you feel the need. It will open any darkness.'

They parted unsentimentally, knowing that they should never see each other again.

They held each other for a long time in an embrace of recognition. But it was clear to both of them that Mariam was no longer the same sister who had left her childhood home ten years earlier, just as Lazarus was no longer the same brother as the one she had parted from. Her return had created great joy and Lazarus had begun immediately to arrange a welcome party, worthy of a queen. Only Mariam's dignified firmness had kept Lazarus from it. Instead, they were now standing in their father's old room at the exact same spot by the window where long ago Lazarus had informed her about the plans for her education.

In spite of the fact that they were both dressed in white, he in the dress of the Brotherhood and she in that of the Therapists, everything that had happened in the meantime lay between them like an impassable chasm. Behind Lazarus' strained attempt to maintain the authoritative front of a patriarch, Mariam saw a joyless human being whose course in life had brought him to a dead end. One single look into her brother's inner life sufficed. Lazarus was an unbalanced person – an instrument out of tune.

'You have arrived in the nick of time,' he said. 'The Romans have tightened their hold on our country. The new prefect is merciless. Even the members of the council of the Sanhedrin in Jerusalem are losing privileges they have had for years. You must go to Capernaum where you are expected. Great things have happened lately and no one knows where it will all end.'

'What things?'

'Something happened which no one could have predicted. Something which will make our relationship with the

Brothers of Qumran and the priests of Jerusalem more difficult than it already is.'

His words were falling over each other like drunken sailors on a binge. Mariam tried to keep his attention, but in vain. She then cut through to the heart of the matter:

'Where is he?'

The question seemed to disconcert Lazarus even more, as if he had totally forgotten the reason for Mariam's return.

'In Capernaum, I presume.'

'Now, tell me what happened.'

She put a hand on his shoulder in order to calm him down. The gesture seemed to have the desired effect. He sat down heavily on their father's old Syrian chair. Then he pulled himself together:

'You have probably heard that the Brothers of Qumran have a candidate, Yohannan, the one called the Baptist. He has been moving about by the delta of the River Jordan, preaching and prophesying. He is baptizing anyone who wants it. No one knew at first that he was the candidate of the Brotherhood. He attracts big crowds indeed. So big in fact that both the Romans and the members of the Sanhedrin have visited him in order to question him about his background and lineage. They asked him if he was the prophet that everyone has been expecting, and he replied evasively in spite of the fact that no one escapes his doomsday prophecies. It has created quite a stir.'

Mariam knew nothing about this Yohannan.

'What is the problem?' she asked impatiently.

It was obvious that Lazarus was trying hard to keep his grip on the story, and Mariam sensed that there was more to it than her brother understood.

'Three months ago Yeshua came back from his long journey to the East. To everyone's dismay, he did not go to the Brotherhood at Carmel as expected, but directly to Capernaum where he has gathered a group of followers around him. He goes about in Galilee speaking to the people. Rumour has it that his audience is growing day by day. A month ago he visited Yohannan in order to be baptized. Rumour now has it that even Yohannan recognizes Yeshua as the expected Messiah. All this has caused both sections of the Brotherhood to become confused and in conflict with each other. Both their respective candidates have failed. It is a serious situation. The Romans and the Sanhedrin on the other hand are worried about the influence that both Yohannan and Yeshua have over people. Yeshua's relatives are worried as well. They say that he has changed so much that even his mother, Mariyam, can hardly recognize him any more. That is why she went to the Brothers of Carmel to make them inform you that the time has come to redeem the covenant. She is hoping that the wedding will return her son to her.'

'Tell me Lazarus, how has Yeshua failed?'

'You know the prophecies and the expectations of the Brotherhood. We are living in those times that the old prophets talked about and the two chosen ones, Yeshua and Yohannan, were considered for the roles of Messiah-the-King and Messiah-the-Priest. They wanted to avoid bad blood between the groups in this way. And then all this happens. Yohannan does not want any superior power. And they say that Yeshua is more interested in fighting the Romans than in fulfilling his destiny.'

'Who can predict the destiny of Yeshua with any certainty?'

Mariam walked to the window and looked across the fields of her childhood. It struck her that they were no longer as well kept as she remembered them.

The following day Mariam and her young guide were on their way to the north. On the way she noticed that Lazarus had been correct in his statement about the Romans: the roads were alive with occupying troops. The soldiers stopped and questioned everybody who looked the slightest bit suspicious. The road between Jerusalem and Jericho was more or less decorated with *tau* crosses carrying the victims of the atrocities of the Romans as a deterrent to others who might harbour the slightest thought of rebellion. The situation did not get any better until Mariam got to Scythopolis at the Gilboa Mountain, where it seemed normal again. There were still lots of soldiers about, but the atmosphere seemed less aggressive. She felt a sense of relief when finally she saw Philoteria and the Sea of Galilee, which reminded her of Mareotis. The cool breeze from the lake cheered her up and she shook her cloak free from all that had been troubling her. When Lamu guided her into the town to find shelter they saw that the place was in great uproar. Groups of townsfolk were standing in the streets talking agitatedly, and it was only the presence of the Roman soldiers that prevented the verbal anxiety from developing into something worse. Mariam stopped at the square and asked Lamu to find out what was going on. Meanwhile, she drank some water from the town well. Here she overheard a conversation between two Pharisees:

'He is a disgrace to his brothers and a dangerous man for the people. He is a swindler leading Israel directly to the slaughter,' an elderly man from the priesthood was shouting.

The other one, a tall, stooping youth, was slightly more favourable:

'Well, sometimes he might be raving but he is of the lineage of David and thus the rightful King of Israel. With the Sanhedrin in Jerusalem as a buffer between him and Pilate, his temper might just hold the Roman judiciary at bay. Then life in this country would be tolerable once more. We don't need those damned Herodians, who are getting fat at the expense of the people and rubbing shoulders with Rome.'

Lamu returned and Mariam had to know right away:

'What has happened?'

'He was here. Yeshua was here and spoke to the people. They say that the audience was so large that the whole square was filled with people. People everywhere, in the trees and on the roofs, just to catch a glimpse of him.'

'What do they say about him?'

'That varies. Some say that he is a false prophet while others see him as the future King of Israel.'

'When was he here?'

'He left yesterday.'

'Where did he go?'

'One man saw him and a few of his closest disciples walking in the direction of Mount Tabor, while others say that he is on his way to Capernaum by way of Hippos on the eastern shores of the lake. That is where his followers are going.'

They walked through the town to the small harbour. Mariam looked over the Sea of Galilee. With her mind she tried to understand what kind of forces were driving the man to whom she had been betrothed. She knew in her heart who he was, but she also knew that he was still looking for a standpoint. In her mind's eye, she saw his melancholy face, which sometimes gave him a peaceful countenance but at other times a haunting look. She knew that his time had come, that his destiny was growing in him already. She realized that at this exact moment he would be torn between two opposite forces, threatening to destroy him if he didn't soon decide which one he would choose. She saw him followed by great throngs of people who tried to get closer, wanting to

174

touch him – and she saw how desperately he wanted and was looking for solitude.

A storm was brewing in the east. White foam blew across the surface of the water. Mariam shook herself. It was time.

Mariam and Lamu rode out towards Mount Tabor the following morning. The mountain showed itself against the sky on the horizon. They were on their way before the sun had gained power. They found two primitive cabins at the foot of the mountain. Two figures dressed in white were seen sitting in the shade in a small palm grove not far away, absorbed in conversation. Mariam asked Lamu to wait for her while she steered her horse in the direction of the two figures.

The two men stood up and looked at her suspiciously. One of them, a big, weather-beaten man with coarse features, took one step towards her.

'Woman, what are you doing here?'

The man's voice sounded gruff and unwelcoming. Mariam saw right through him. She smiled:

'I'm looking for the Chosen One.'

Mariam's direct answer made the man uneasy. Then he replied,

'What do you know about this?'

Now Mariam also looked closely at the other man.

He was finer built and had beautiful, almost female features. The smile he gave was reserved. Then he said,

'What is your name, woman?'

'You'll know my name soon enough. I have something very important to hand over to your rabbi and would be happy to know where I can find him.'

It was the squarely built man who answered:

'Just give us what you brought, and we shall pass it on to him.'

Mariam sat silently in her saddle. A fly buzzed through the air. It landed on the man's forehead. Mariam waited until the man had tried to swat the fly, which he missed. Then she said,

'What I have to pass on is more fleeting than a fly and yet greater than the greatest of anything you'll ever be able to imagine.'

Mariam's words made the man frown. Who did she think she was? He realized that he couldn't put her off so easily. Her steadfast composure made him uneasy. Mariam pulled at the reins and turned around.

'Don't trouble yourselves on my account. I'll find him myself.'

She steered the horse toward the path leading up the mountain and started ascending. The sun was high in the sky, sending its remorseless rays over the Holy Land. One of the men shouted something after her but the words disappeared in the vibrating dry haze.

She hadn't been riding for long when she saw the cabin. It was even simpler than the two at the foot of the mountain. Apparently, nobody was near and she took it for granted that he was either in the cabin or had gone further up. She tied the horse to a tree and walked to the entrance of the cabin. It was dark inside and her eyes had to adjust to it after the bright sunlight. Then she could see the outline of a man lying curled up on his side on the ground. She bent her head and stepped inside. It was him. He looked as if he were sleeping. Two lines on the dust-covered skin under one of his eyes told her that he had been crying. She stood for a moment watching him. She then kneeled down next to him, leaned forward and kissed him on his forehead.

Shortly afterwards, she was on her way down the mountain.

'Where are we going?' Lamu asked as they rode north.

'To Capernaum,' she answered lost in her own thoughts.

Capernaum was festival-clad and the streets were filled with expectant people who had come from near and far to listen to the prophet who, according to the rumour, was the long-expected Messiah and the rightful King. Lamu immediately wanted to bring Mariam to the house of Mariyam, but Mariam preferred to find a more neutral place. They had the good fortune to find an inn on the outskirts of the town. It was almost impossible to find a vacancy for miles and whoever wanted to could let out a sleeping mat for a shekel.

The festivities started in the afternoon. The street vendors got very busy when people started flocking into the town. The streets were so full that it was difficult to get anywhere, while the rumours said that Yeshua was seen both here and there. The town was boiling over with pent-up expectations when suddenly a sigh went through the crowd. Mariam let herself be drawn along by the throng of people between the houses, while children and young men jumped from roof to roof. The prophet had asked people to convene at the square in front of the synagogue.

The square was alive with people. Yeshua himself was standing on a platform.

Behind him the light from the setting sun shone dramatically highlighting his aura. It was a different man Mariam saw standing there than the one curled up sleeping whom she had kissed on the forehead the day before. Now he stood poised, looking over the crowd. He had a long beard and long brown hair down to his shoulders. He wore the traditional white coat of the Brotherhood. A handful of men dressed similarly had made a ring around him in order to keep the keenest ones at a distance. Now Mariam saw that there were two women in the circle just below Yeshua and she assumed that one of them was Yeshua's mother, Mariyam.

Suddenly people grew silent. Yeshua greeted the crowd by raising his hand.

'Peace be with you.'

His voice was warm and clear. But it was still difficult to hear everything he said. However, Mariam understood that he was talking about an angel who had been sent ahead in order to prepare the way for the one who would come, and that this angel was Yohannan the Baptist.

'But to what can I compare the people of this generation? What do they look like? They look like children sitting in the square yelling at each other: we played the flute for you and you didn't dance, we sang dirges and you didn't cry. Hear Ye, Yohannan the Baptist has come, he neither eats bread nor drinks wine and you say: he is possessed. And the Son of Man has come, he both eats and drinks and you say: see that glutton and that drunk, friend of publicans and sinners. But wisdom has conquered through its children.'

Mariam soon understood that it wasn't necessarily the content of the speech which went straight to the hearts of people but rather the intensity with which it was said. Standing there, caressed by the last rays of the sun, he really was the Messiah incarnate, king of the people and the foundation stone of faith. All were spellbound at this moment. Even the most hardened would put his life in the hands of this man without hesitation. He gave the people new hope. Not about anything in particular. Rather the feeling that in general better times were on the way. But still, something was missing. Mariam was suffused suddenly by a feeling of loneliness. She suddenly doubted the man to whom she had been betrothed. In spite of his courage in speaking against Rome she noticed the fear behind the words and the assumed manliness, which wasn't real but simply a pose to which he was clinging in order to go through with his mission. Standing right there, radiating and apparently approachable, she sensed an invisible distance, which at least to her made him seem dishonest. She saw how eagerly his disciples tried to keep people at bay, and before anyone knew it he was gone again, as suddenly as he had arrived, leaving a hungry throng of people behind.

When darkness fell there was singing and dancing going on in the town. Rumours said that Mariyam, the mother of the prophet, was celebrating in his honour at the home of one of the most esteemed Pharisees of the town. These rumours were the source of much confusion since this Pharisee was well known for his readiness to meet the wishes of the Roman authorities. How could Yeshua dine with such people?

Mariam moved about in a state of trance. She only saw and heard what was absolutely essential. At another level she knew very well what she had to do. With Lamu's help she visited the stalls of the merchants in order to buy the remaining things she needed: cinnamon bark, sweet-flag oil, cassia and aloe. She tried to find out where she could get the best olive oil. When she had finished her shopping they returned to the inn. Behind the building was a yard where the local winemaker used to work. Here Mariam mixed the ingredients with the myrrh she had received from Salome. She was ready an hour later. In the meantime she had Lamu find out where the party for Yeshua was held. There was no time to waste.

They easily found the house. Many from the crowd had settled there, waiting for something to happen. Mariam worked her way through them with Lamu following closely behind her. Two of Yeshua's disciples stood at the door.

'What are you doing here, woman?'

Mariam answered behind her veil:

'I have something very important to give to Rabbi Yeshua.'

One of the men was about to push her back but the other moved between them. It was the same man with the feminine features that Mariam had met the previous day at the foot of Mount Tabor.

'Wait,' he almost whispered.

To Mariam he said:

'You can safely give us your gift for the master and we shall pass it on to him.'

He seemed very nervous and Mariam pulled her veil aside:

'Don't bother.'

She briskly stepped between them and went into the house.

Somewhere people were talking in loud voices. She followed the sound and suddenly found herself at the entrance of a large hall where between twenty and thirty people were reclining around a table loaded with food and wine. The men spoke coarsely and laughed. The sight made her sad. This was not the way she had imagined meeting with her betrothed. A tear rolled treacherously down her cheek. She stayed for a while in order to make sure that he was there. Then she spotted Mariyam at the end of the table. Yeshua was at her side. He did not at all look like the future Messiah of Israel as she saw him there.

Nobody took notice of her when she walked across the floor. Not until she was standing right behind Yeshua did one of them look up.

'Who is this woman?'

Now the whole group reacted and they focused their attention on Mariam. Without further ado she knelt down at Yeshua's feet. While opening the alabaster jar her tears ran down and mixed with the content. Slowly she began anointing the feet of Yeshua. She had arrived in the nick of time.

'How dare you – and who gave you permission to carry the gown with our mark on it?' one of the disciples cried out angrily. Mariam recognized the voice.

'Stop her!' the host shouted.

'Let her, Petrus. And also to you Simon do I say: I came to your house. I was not made welcome. But I'm made welcome by this woman. You did not anoint me. But this woman anoints me with her tears. In whatever you may find her guilty, I forgive her every sin. Much shall be the one forgiven who has loved much. Only the holier-than-thou cannot be saved.'

Mariam dried the surplus oil from the feet of Yeshua with her hair. Then she kissed them. A little later she got up. Their eyes met but only for a short moment. She saw something else being born in him. He was bewildered. He looked like someone who didn't know what was up or down. He disappeared into her burning eyes. Who was she?

'I'm the silver cup.'

Did he actually hear her or was this just an erring thought?

He got up and saw her disappearing the same way as she had come. Laughter bellowed behind him.

The silver cup?

What silver cup?

Who was this unusual and beautiful woman?

After that there were rumours about the foreign woman, the sinner, who had the nerve to intrude on the master and without asking anointed his feet. This was totally unheard of. Evil tongues claimed that the woman was a prostitute who had committed many sins. Some even went as far as saying that she had attempted to have an intimate relationship with Yeshua, at the home of Simon the Pharisee and in front of the master's mother and all the other guests. She had kissed his feet. Only a real wife would do that.

In the meantime, Yeshua and his disciples had left Capernaum in order to find solitude in a small abandoned village in a valley close to the Jordan just outside of Bethsaida. So far, Yeshua had refused to continue the campaign planned by Petrus, a journey taking him all over the country and when the time was ripe bringing him victoriously to Jerusalem. Petrus had recognized the woman and he was irritated by the fact that he hadn't succeeded in stopping her once and for all. Especially now, when he saw the effect the episode had on his master.

As the days went by it became clear that something had happened which could not be dismissed too easily. Yeshua was silent and distanced himself from the disciples. Anyone could see that he wasn't himself. It finally became too much even for Petrus. He went to Yeshua, who was sitting in the shade of a palm tree.

'Master, what is bothering you?'

Yeshua didn't move and didn't answer.

'You haven't eaten anything and you haven't spoken for three days. This must stop now.' But Yeshua didn't answer, he was in another world.

Mariam and Lamu waited at the inn until peace ruled in the town once more. The owners of the inn began to feel rather uncomfortable about their staying there. Lamu tried to get Mariam to visit Mariyam's house but her mind was elsewhere. She sensed that what must happen would happen.

This was realized on the fourth day. The disciple with the female features, Thomas, was in Capernaum with another disciple, Yuda, in order to find the woman who had created such a hiatus.

When they entered the courtyard, Mariam sat in deep contemplation. This didn't seem to bother the two of them. It was clear that they were in a hurry.

'Woman, the master wants to see you.'

Mariam opened her eyes. Without answering, she stood up and straightened her gown. Lamu was already busy packing. Half an hour later they were on their way.

The moment of truth. Exactly as predicted. His time and her time were near. Only the circumstances were different. If she had known them beforehand she wasn't so sure that she would have taken the task upon herself. She was no longer the young girl in love, who dreamed of marriage and love – who once dreamt such passionate dreams about this man. She now just wanted it to be over, no matter what the forthcoming meeting would bring.

They rode into the abandoned village three hours later.

11

The phone rang.

It was the radio and television journalist Anders Laugesen who invited me to participate in a television programme about travelling as a pilgrim. I could more or less decide the destinations. The only problem was that it was planned to be on the air a few months later, which meant that we had to leave as soon as possible. In spite of the fact that I was quite busy I heard myself answering very clearly and unreservedly with a YES! I suppose that something in my subconscious must have been waiting for a new way for my ongoing search to show itself. This was it. Immediately after that decision had been taken it became equally clear that the journey should go to the Middle East, Syria, Jordan and Israel. Anders and I would travel by train from Denmark to Istanbul in Turkey and then on to Syria from whence we would continue by car.

The whole trip was planned to take three weeks. When I told the Seer about these plans, he said in his usual dry way:

'Have a nice trip. An initiation is awaiting you close to Damascus.'

Unfortunately, the prolonged crisis between Israel and Palestine escalated to such a degree that it was decided that the expedition should go only to Syria. This decision would later prove to be more than fortunate.

Anders and I boarded the train at Aarhus Central Station on a cloudy September day. We had purposely been placed at each end of the train to give us the opportunity of going on pilgrimage 'alone'. Anders brought his digital camera and his tape recorder so that we could produce sections of the programme on the way, whenever the opportunity was there. The real cameraman of the programme would fly to Damascus five days later.

It is unbelievable what such a train journey can do. It is one of the most effective tools if you want to get rid of your rigid, civilized defences. We changed trains in Cologne and began the long, tiring journey through Eastern Europe: Hungary, Rumania and Bulgaria. We rattled slowly into a depressing hopelessness, which apparently had no end. Layer after layer we had to lay aside our own desperate attempts to repress the kind of inner poverty we met each time we were tempted to defend our own limitations. It is the kind of poverty which always feels cheated, which feels that it hasn't received what was promised or what it really deserved. This happens as soon as we enter the land of misers, where no one can get enough and where only the strongest survive. Far too much in Eastern Europe is a reflection of our own inner poverty. We have let ourselves become blinded by external values and all kinds of unimportant luxury. It is the kind of poverty, which has everything, but only wants that which supplies the illusions about an eternal, painless life at the top, where nothing moves and everything remains as it was. It is the kind of poverty, which is forced to barricade itself in seedy, first-class compartments at night, for fear of being robbed, without any kind of sustenance and in the ever-present stench of decay and urine. This is where, in the course of a few days, you have no choice but to face your own naked existence, the skeletons in the cupboard and the numerous unseen scars on your mind.

The arrival at Istanbul foreboded a change. We were on our way into a lighter atmosphere. We had a single overnight stay in the city before continuing by train to Aleppo in Syria and, right from the railway station, the doors opened to another sphere. Anders noticed a poster saying that a so-called *sema* (a Sufi dance ritual) would be held in one of the old railway station halls that very evening, where dervishes from Mevlana Rumi's Sufi order were going to dance. We immediately booked tickets for this occasion, which turned out to be a genuine rarity.

Rumi, who was born in Afghanistan in 1207 but lived in Turkey from 1215 until his death in 1273, more than any other has become synonymous with the Sufis. He is one of the most treasured poets of the Sufi tradition, and his importance goes far beyond the Muslim world. Rumi is the indisputable master of love-alchemy par excellence. We therefore arrived at the *sema* brimming with expectation, and we noticed that about fifty people were already present.

A band, a *mutrip,* a group of five musicians, played for about half an hour before six dervishes, three men and three women, took over the floor. The participation of women was not only a surprise but a historic event since this kind of dance had for centuries only been for men.

The dervishes wear a special kind of costume representing the death of the little self. The characteristic, pipe-like hat called the *sikke* is literally the tombstone of the ego, while the *hirka*, a long, black cloak, represents the grave itself.

The atmosphere was intense as the dervishes stepped into the circle with their arms crossed. This is how the unity with God is reflected. Then they started the first circle of the dance, consisting of four circles altogether.

With their arms stretched out on each side, the right hand opening upwards and the left downwards, the dancers now turned about in faster and faster spirals. The position of the hands represent the central part of the ritual which expresses the sentence: '*We receive from God, We give to humanity, we keep nothing for ourselves.*'

The expression 'dervish' in itself means to die. This not only symbolizes the ideal of poverty stemming from the days when the dervishes had to go begging from door to door; it also symbolises the modern dervish endeavouring to be a door, or channel, between God and people.

They now turned about themselves and around each other just like the planets of the solar system, changing the room into a rotating galaxy of love and light. It was unbelievably exalting being a witness to this ritual, which was performed with such dignity and humility that it was impossible not to be very moved by it. Not only did we witness an intimate act – but everybody who saw it became part of a greater transformation. Each movement was dedicated to us.

Sufism has always been seen as the mystical side of Islam, and its history has therefore always been officially considered identical with the history of Islam, starting at the beginning of the tenth century.

The word *Sufi* may be translated as *pure wool* or *those dressed in wool* or *those dressed in white*. It was a term used

about itinerant sages, dressed in simple woollen cloaks. There are also certain language ties between *Sufi* and the Greek word *sophia*, wisdom or certainty. These itinerant sages weren't interested in politics or religion. For them the relationship with God was one of love, which was solely about dissolving your personality so that the soul could reunite with its Father. That is why these Sufis always submitted to the ruling power. This was the only way in which they could get close peacefully to the goal they aspired to. Some mystics claim that it is almost a coincidence that the Sufis are a part of Islam and follow the law of the Koran, while others claim that it is precisely the Prophet Mohammed and his Koran, which made these sages choose Islam.

The true Sufis feel that all the great religions of the world and all the mystical traditions share the same essential truth. They believe in one God and that this one God is behind everything, seen as well as unseen. You do not have to go to Mecca or to Jerusalem in order to find your God, He lives in your heart. Life doesn't end with death. Life in this world is like a dream, while true life is in the next world. It is important to the Sufis to be present in the world with all that this entails of work, marriage and other worldly obligations. But for them it is about deifying their everyday life, about living a normal life in a very special way. Being *in* the world, but also understanding that you are not *of* it.

In the evening, after the moving experience with the dance of the dervishes, I began thinking about the idea that maybe the first Sufis had been the group of itinerant mystics bearing the name of Those Dressed in White. Was it in reality their traditions which had formed the foundation of the well-known Middle Eastern and Persian traditions such as Judaism, Christianity and Islam? The Sufis' preferences among holy books were and still are the Torah of Moses, the Psalms of David, The Gospels of Yeshua and the Koran of Mohammed. Their love tradition contains a very strong female aspect. They have kept this fire burning for centuries and inspired mystics everywhere. Imagine if this was the tradition from which Mariam really came – and in which she disappeared again?

We boarded the Syria Express the following day, which turned out to be a slow train taking us through ninety towns in Turkey to Aleppo in Syria, at the speed of thirty kilometres an hour, where we were collected by our driver, Ahmad, and safely brought to our base, a small family-run hotel, Afamia, in Damascus.

Our arrival in Syria was in many ways a homecoming. In spite of the many unfamiliar problems apparent in modern Syria, such as the fact that the country is a police state, it still felt more open. The poverty here does not breed inhospitability and egocentricity as the spiritual poverty of the Western World seems to.

Syria is an Arabian nation. Sunni and Shia Muslims, Ishmaelites, Druses and Alawite Muslims live side by side with Christians from such different Churches as Greek Orthodox, Armenian Orthodox, Syrian Orthodox, Syrian Catholic, Greek Catholic, Roman Catholic and Maronite, as well as a minority of Jews who live here without the problems that are inevitable in other countries.

Arriving in Damascus was like falling into a boiling pot of strange smells, colours, noise, warmth and religion, all of which were covered by a reeking layer of diesel fuel. Stepping into this age-old city, which may be the oldest inhabited city in the world, is like stepping into a room where some of mankind's oldest archetypes lie hidden. The unfamiliar mysticism, which is obvious to any newcomer, is both seducing and frightening because it is so intense and deep.

The unreserved submission reigning here is a threat to any cool and detached attitude and, if you insist on retaining this, there are other places in the world more appropriate for playing tourist.

I found myself in a state of mind where any kind of defence had crumbled and I felt like an open book. The foundation for such openness was basically the hardship of travel as well as the challenging diet. This meant that I was more than usually sensitive and sharp. I had found before that such a state of mind makes it easier for me to step into the stream, going with the flow instead of against it. When you are in that state of mind all your old patterns of habit seem psychotic and caricature-like. This state of mind calls for your total sense of humour without which it becomes unbearable. Luckily I was in light-hearted company making any kind of self-righteousness or self-pity impossible.

On the way to Damascus we visited the monastery built to commemorate Simon the Pillar Saint. Furthermore, we visited the fantastic castle Crac des Chevaliers built by the Templars during the crusades. We spent the night in the desert monastery *Deir Mar Musa al-Habashi* where a former Jesuit priest, Father Paolo, had created an unorthodox monastery, which was more like a Dutch hippy commune than it was a serious abbey or nunnery. We went to the great Umayyad mosque where they keep the relics of John the Baptist and where I was blessed by a blind Sufi master. In Ma'alouda I met some of the few Aramaic-speaking people. We were invited to service and tea by the archbishops of the Syrian Orthodox Church, who had arrived at the St Ephrem Monastery from all over the world to participate in the annual synod, which was held the very day we visited here.

We were now on our way to the largest convent in Syria, Our Lady of Saydnaya. It was a very hot afternoon and we drove through a desert area to the north of Damascus. I was in a state of deep open being and felt that something was changing inside me. The veritable bombardment of spirituality and religious symbols, which we met everywhere, had opened the same layers in me. The seriousness and dedication shown by the practitioners of the various traditions, Muslim as well as Christian, was stimulating to our own introspection. The daily practice of prayers became more and more intense as the days passed by, and I started sensing some of the deeper secrets behind the mystery of prayer. As a result of my prayers, I started feeling the presence of Mariam and faintly sensing the Voice:

'*Prayers are not for the sake of God. They are for the sake of people. They are an awakening of all our resources. Through the medium of prayer you get into a state of mind enabling you to get in contact with the higher levels, the higher Self. When you personify God through your prayers, you are praying from the little self. No doubt, it has a certain effect, but a limited one only. When you understand that God is not a person but a creating power with an identity, which is only personified through your creation, you suddenly understand that the only form of blasphemy possible is made by the one who is praying to a personified God, the picture of Whom is created by you. Praying to such a god is limiting to the Power.*'

The car was jumping along on the bumpy road. In front of us the impressive Saydnaya Convent was faintly seen on the horizon. We were on our way there in order to participate in the annual festival in honour of the Convent's famous Mary-icon, *Shaghoura*, which simply means 'known' or 'famous'. The icon is a copy of one of the four icons, which the evangelist Luke is said to have painted. The icon has miraculous powers. Stories are told about pilgrims who have come close to it and who have been healed by it. On the day of the annual festival it is said to have a positive influence on women who cannot have children. The women then stay overnight at the convent and it is said that 90 per cent of them regain their fertility. According to legend the convent is built on the site where Noah planted his vines after the Flood.

There were people everywhere when we arrived, and most of them were women who were staying overnight at the monastery. Every square yard of the long passages was covered with mattresses and bed linen. A group of Bedouin women had already started the festivities in one of the passages and those who passed them by were pulled into the dance. An elderly woman caught me by my arm and heaved me up into the air. I was taken completely by surprise and must have looked rather comical. She put me down again but kept her grip on my hand while she started a series of movements which looked very much like a fertility ritual. The other women formed a circle around us while they articulated a series of howls. There was no escaping it. It all happened so fast that I had no time at all to reflect on the situation. It was a veritable attack on my aloofness and autonomous state of mind. I had either to let go or look like a self-righteous sour-face, who was sufficient to himself and his own spirituality. There was a short struggle before I surrendered unconditionally to the dancing and howling of the women. I danced more that evening than I have danced for years.

Thus freed of my final and frayed defences, I slipped into the flow of people on their way to the Holy of Holies. It is no coincidence that the entrance to the small room, where *The Blessed Madonna* is hanging, is so low that you have to bend your knees in order to get in. The body position equals the inner attitude you must take when you are in the room where so many pilgrims have prayed and surrendered themselves.

The room is filled with candles and you cannot stay there for long before a fire is ignited in your heart. No matter which denomination you belong to you cannot help being moved by this place where so much hope is being expressed. Here Muslim and Jew are queuing up next to Christians. Here man is one before the One and Only.

After a short meditation at the icon I stepped into the flow of people once more, leading me through an opening at the other end of the room. In the passage between the icon room and the convent church some sisters dressed in black were handing out small envelopes containing candle wicks to the pilgrims. Moving along in the queue I was still in a contemplative state of mind. My heart was totally open. A deep feeling of unrestrained acceptance bubbled up through me and put me in a frame of mind that I can only describe with the rather trite word: *happiness*. Unlike anything I had formerly experienced as happiness, this feeling sprang from a being deep inside of me, which I can only describe as *the eternal being*.

There was a bend in the passage, and I had just turned the corner and ended my Aramaic prayer when a sudden impulse made me look to the left. In the shadow on the wall was a small, humble, red and golden icon depicting Madonna with the Infant Yeshua. For reasons I still cannot explain, I stepped out of the queue in order to study the icon more closely. It turned out to be what I call a vulgar-icon, which simply means that the icon is a reproduction. I just stood there for a long time studying the icon, which did not differ from the other icons in the monastery except for the fact that it was a reproduction. But there was still something about it, which made me want to spend the rest of the evening in its vicinity. The room in which the icon was hanging was filled with an indefinable kind of energy, and I imagined that this was due to the thousands of pilgrims who had passed along this passage for hundreds of years feeling the same kind of happiness that I was feeling. There was a sense of release in the room.

I stayed in front of the icon for three hours. And suddenly I saw it. Suddenly I could see the symbolism which was very obvious but which had been hidden from me to begin with.

The picture itself was fractured and the line of fracture ran directly through the solar plexus of the Madonna. Her left hand, carrying the child, was below the line, while her right hand in front of her heart was above the line. I was lost in this symbolism when Anders and Jeppe arrived. They wanted a few shots with me commenting on my experiences. We had just finished this when the head of the convent, Sister Theodora, came in together with another sister and turned directly to me. Sister Theodora looked closely at me as if she wanted to make sure that I was sincere. At least, this was how it seemed to me. There was no doubt that she could see what state of mind I was in. She then lifted the icon from its nail on the wall, kissed it and blessed it and handed it to me.

There.

Just like that.

We were all speechless. Sister Theodora broke the silence:

'We found the picture in a corner here in this passage about fifty years ago. Someone must have dropped it or thrown it here. A young novice repaired it and made this beautiful icon. The icon is called *Our Lady of the Broken Hearted*. It has been hanging at this spot all these years. Take good care of her. Wherever you take her, she'll look after you.'

The sisters then disappeared. They had plenty to do. That is why it was completely incomprehensible that they had noticed my infatuation with the icon. A young sister, who

'Our Lady of the Broken Hearted'

followed us to the car, gave me the last blessing, which left me stunned:

'I think you ought to know, that the novice who prepared the icon fifty years ago was in fact Sister Theodora herself.'

On returning to Damascus in the car I noticed that the hands of the Madonna were placed in almost the same pose as those of the dervishes when they are dancing. The message for present and future light workers was clear:

'We receive from God, We give to humanity, We keep nothing for ourselves.'

I hardly slept that night but sat in front of the icon, which I had placed on a shelf in my hotel room. It took a while before I understood the value of the gift I had received from the nuns at Saydnaya. But also the responsibility accompanying it. It was as if a pact had been made. I now had to take upon me what was mine to do. The moment had come when I had to understand that the time for my eternal excuses was over.

The pact was confirmed two days later when we visited the stigmatized Myrna from Soufanieh.

The Nazzour family live in a small two-storey house in Soufanieh, a suburb of Damascus. Myrna was eighteen years old when suddenly oil seeped from her hands during a visit to her sister-in-law who was ill. It turned out that the oil had healing powers. A small vulgar-icon, which she got from her husband, also began seeping oil. Shortly after she had a series of Virgin Mary revelations in which she received various messages. Since 1983 she has experienced several ecstasies during which she has repeatedly become marked with the stigmata. The events have officially been accepted as true miracles and pilgrims come each year from all over the world to pray and to participate in the Masses held at her house.

We arrived on the afternoon of 11 September. There were only a few pilgrims in the room that was used for prayers by the visitors. Myrna was dressed in a simple, black dress. In spite of the disturbance created by the preparations for the filming of the ceremony I could see the activity of light around her. The lucidity of her eyes was not of this world, and I knew that she was looking into a reality where work was being done to correct everything that the rest of us were busy destroying.

I had brought my icon in the hope that Myrna would bless it. The bustle around us continued and it didn't get any better when the shooting of the film began.

After the interview, which took place through the assistance of an interpreter, since Myrna's English was rather limited, we walked into the small chapel on the first floor where Myrna prayed for a short while. I was standing immediately behind her while she prayed her Syrian prayers, and I noticed how the activity of light around her intensified. I was affected so much by this that it was difficult for me to stifle the bubbling pleasure within me, which threatened to disturb the divine service with an uncontrollable laughter. When she had finished and held the icon to her mouth in order to kiss it, she looked very surprised and said in her broken English:

'Oh, it smells of flowers.'

She handed me the icon so that I could smell the delicious smell of flowers coming from the picture. A little later the smell extended to the rest of the room. We were all overwhelmed and deeply touched.

When I was saying goodbye to Myrna she pointed to the icon in my plastic bag and said:

Myrna of Soufanieh in Damascus

'Take good care of her. She takes good care of you.'

I nodded and blurted out, 'I will.' If I had been in doubt before, then I certainly wasn't now.

As if this wasn't enough, the Board of Directors upstairs apparently had decided that I was somewhat dense, and they wanted to make sure that I understood the message. The night before my departure, during my usual astral outing, I met a radiating ball waiting for me in one of the lower regions. As I confronted the ball it changed and took the shape of the star of Mariam, a six-pointed hexagram. I didn't take much notice of this event apart from the joy in still being able to get in contact with this kind of energy. I woke up early next morning and decided to take a walk in the souk in the old part of Damascus. Most of the stalls were still closed and there were not many people about. I walked about at random until suddenly a man called out to me in a part of the city that I didn't know. He asked me what I was looking for. Without thinking about it I just answered that I was looking for antiques. Shortly after he led me into a passage and knocked on the door of a posh restaurant. A man in a lounge suit opened the door and invited us in. The restaurant also turned out to be a similarly posh antique shop with display cases between the tables. Without asking what I was looking for the proprietor went to one of the cases, opened it and took out a round metal plate with a grip on the back of it. When he placed it on the glass counter in front of me I was rather dumbfounded. The star of Mariam was etched on the metal plate. Arabic characters were written around it and I could see that they were laterally reversed.

'What is this?' I asked, speechless.

'This is a 500-year-old seal which the Sufi sheikhs used to stamp on the white gowns of their pupils when they had served their apprenticeships.'

Sufi seal of Damascus, circa 1500 AD

Until this day I do not know how this man could know that this seal meant something to me. But I have no doubt that the Board of Directors upstairs had something to do with it.

Later that day I started my return trip by train, the same way as I had come and all by myself. It went very well until I got to the Central Station in Bucharest. I had two and a half hours to wait and as soon as I stepped into the arrival hall I was approached by two uniformed security guards. They were very obliging and asked me where I came from and where I was going. They found out about the time of departure and which platform for me. Then they told me that for my own security it was absolutely essential that they stay with me until my departure. I didn't understand the reason for this and tried to tell them that. They insisted. Two and a half hours later they followed me to the train and into my compartment. I felt rather nervous about it and hung on to my precious icon, which I carried under my left arm, and my equally precious Sufi seal which I carried under my right arm, holding the remainder of my luggage in my hands.

Then it came cold and clear:

'You must pay for security.'

I was hardly surprised at the words.

'I haven't ordered any kind of security,' I said calmly.

There was no apparent reaction.

'You must pay for security, one hundred euros.'

Thoughts were rushing through my head.

'I have neither dollars nor euros, only this,' I said knowing that both my dollars and euros were safe in my money belt.

I let one of my bags slide to the floor and took out a handful of Rumanian notes from a side pocket in my trousers.

He gave the money a quick glance. Then he knocked my arm away, lifted my shirt, unzipped my money belt and in one sweep took all my currency, and holding it into the air he said:

'Then this is nothing, eh? Have a nice trip.'

Then they turned about and left.

I immediately sat down and started laughing. Of course I was somewhat shaken. And then again I wasn't. I had no doubt at all that this was the final lesson. It was about values. The robber had underlined it so heavily that even I couldn't help seeing it. The money was nothing. I was bringing back the real value.

12

Yeshua sat watching a cat, which had jumped into the room through a hole in the roof in the house where he had just spent three days and nights. Yeshua had lost all sense of motivation after meeting the unknown young woman. The path he was on and, even more, the goals and hopes the brothers had on his behalf, had suddenly lost all meaning. The event had also created a disturbance among the brothers. But his mother, if possible, was even more agitated than all of them put together. She had kept on about the young woman, Mariam from Bethany, to whom he had been betrothed ten years earlier, and who was now on her way to Capernaum in order to fulfil her part of the pact. That is why the incident with this sinful woman came at a very bad time. Yeshua had dismissed his mother but with the result that she simply kept bothering him even more. Only Yohannan understood the implications of what had happened. His heart had also been touched by the actions of this foreign woman.

The cat was licking its fur when suddenly it froze at the sound of steps outside the house. Yeshua sat up. Not a sound. What was going on? The meeting with this woman had turned everything upside down. The power she had displayed in just a short instant was of a totally different dimension than the kind with which you seduce the masses. She was of another world. Was she one of the temptations of Satan, he wondered? She had performed her act with a humble dignity, which spoke against the presence of any kind of will based in a desire for power. Was she an angel sent by the Lord? Yeshua slipped into a dream-world of conflicting thoughts. In a hidden part of his consciousness he heard a voice and felt a strong desire to move in its direction.

'I am the *Shekhinah*. I am stepping into the world in order to reintroduce the truth. I raise the fallen ones, heal the broken ones and bring peace to the persecuted ones. I defy the lie and offer a new life to people. Drink from my stream and you shall never be thirsty again. Unite with me and the eternal life is yours.'

The woman, that he hadn't been able to get out of his mind since the day she had anointed his feet, was now standing in front of him. A light radiated from her, emphasizing both her heavenly and diabolically seductive beauty. Her eyes were like fire burning into his. The cat nestled against her legs.

Yeshua sat rooted to the spot. The young woman let her cloak slip to the earth floor.

'I was sent here by the Force. I come to those who are able to receive me. I am found by those who seek me out. Look at me, you who seek to unite with me. Hear me, you who listen. You who await me, absorb my essence. Do not forget me for I am the first one and the last one.'

She loosened the laces of her gown, opened it in front and bared her breasts to him. It happened so fast and took him so much by surprise that he lost his breath. The sight made him sick with lust. He had never seen such a beautiful being.

'I am honoured and I'm ostracized. I am the whore and the holy one. I am the wife and the virgin. I am the mother and the daughter. I am the heavenly bride for whom there is no husband to be found. My power is of the one who sent me.'

She loosened the last laces, let her gown slide down and stood completely naked in front of him.

'I am the incomprehensible silence. I am the voice, the sound of which is manifold. I am the everlasting word. I am the blessing of my own name. I am wisdom and ignorance. I am shameless and I am shameful. I am strength; I am fear. I am peace and I am war. I am the void in fullness. I am the one and only in emptiness. I dissolve all concepts and all images. That is why I am limitless. That is why I am everything. Do not forget me, for I am the ostracized one and the long-awaited one.'

He could wait no longer. He had to posses this divine being. She laid herself on the bed made by the cloak and the white gown. Yeshua felt faint. The words of the woman kept sounding in his head: 'I am honoured and I'm ostracized. I am the whore and the holy one. I am the wife and the virgin. I am the mother and the daughter. I am the heavenly bride for whom there is no husband to be found.' What did it all mean? He was sick with longing. Then he got up and walked, unsteadily, towards her. He saw her radiating body in the darkness, the goal of his desires, the beloved one, waiting for her lover. He slipped his coat over his head and sank down on the bed next to her. He was like a youth whose lust centred in a curve between his legs. He reached for her breasts and pressed his abdomen towards her, but she put a finger on his lips, and with her other hand she took hold of his erect member holding him in a firm grip, which took him so much by surprise that he groaned aloud. She held him like this without moving until he regained his composure. Still, the pressure was almost unbearable for him. Then she put her mouth close to his ear and whispered:

'Be vigilant, you who are able to listen. Listen, you who have been sent. Listen, you who are awake and risen from sleep. Many are the beautiful shapes making up the great illusion, the empty sin and the fickle lust, which man embraces until he becomes spiritually sober and goes to the meeting place. That is where you'll find me. And when you have found me you shall live, never to taste death again.'

She slowly began massaging him and felt how he was about to burst in her hand. He reached for her breasts again and caressed them and kissed her hard. He had already arrived at the point of no return.

She let him do whatever he wanted to do since she realized that it was impossible to get to him before his wild, sexually guided passion had been released.

He curled up and moaned like a maimed animal. Many years of repressed eros had been set free. Afterwards he lay on his back trying to catch his breath. She stroked his forehead and whispered:

'There are seven doors leading to the true human being. Seven holy centres through which the Holy Power is flowing, uniting with the Universe. The power you have just experienced is just a pale shadow of the Power to which I have been elected to lead you.'

She let him go, got halfway up and knelt at his side. Carefully, she placed her hand on his member and felt how once more it grew between her fingers.

'This door is your biggest hindrance. As it is now, you are

tied to the burden of your ancestors and all the heritage of man – good and bad. But all of this is just a faint reflection of your own fixations and limitations, as well as the fear which makes you forget who you really are.'

He experienced another erection, but now he could both hear and see her, because this time he was not guided by his naked lust. She calmly massaged him with her hand, but it was her words that caressed his heart and nurtured a totally different longing, the direction of which he did not know.

'There is an almost impenetrable darkness behind that door.'

She let go of him and started searching for something in the pocket of the cloak, which made up part of their bed. Yeshua held her back, pulled her down to him and kissed her tenderly and passionately. She let him do it, but still smiling, tore herself away:

'You learn quickly.'

Shortly after she found what she was looking for: the ring, which Salome had given her. She put it on her own finger; the ring finger of her right hand. She then held her hand about ten centimetres above his organ.

'Yohannan baptized you with water. I shall baptize you with fire. The two sapphires of this ring radiate the two poles *Ein Sof* and *Shekhinah* of the Creator YHVH. These two will open any darkness.'

Her hand circled above him in soft movements and he immediately felt his abdomen vibrating.

'Now I'm going to tell you the secret behind the name of the Creator. *Yod* is Wisdom. *He* is Acknowledgement, *Vav* collects six sapphires (*sefirot*) into one: Strength, Grace, Compassion, Radiance, Eternity and the Foundation Stone. The last *He* is *Shekhina* (the royal kingdom of the heavenly bride). *Ein Sof* and *Shekhina* radiate through YHVH

(Yod-he-vav-he/Jehova) in unity. Through the ten sapphires God's Daughter and God's Son are born.'

While Mariam's hand hovered above Yeshua's manhood she put her mouth close to his ear and whispered:

'*Ephatah.* Open up. Release all that has been forgotten. Move all that has stagnated. Let Yodhevavhe's Power flow freely through this door and that darkness. Let go of the command of the lineage deciding who you ought to be, and instead be the one that you really are in your true Self.'

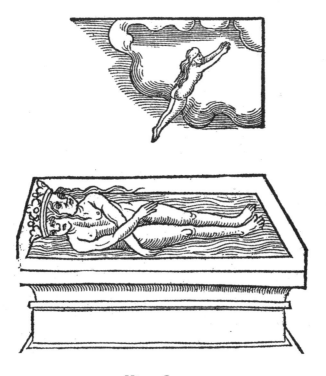

Hieros Gamos
(*Rosarium philosophorum 1550*)

EIN SOF

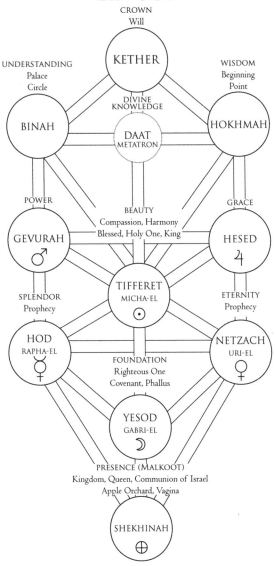

CROWN
Will

KETHER

UNDERSTANDING
Palace
Circle

WISDOM
Beginning
Point

DIVINE
KNOWLEDGE

BINAH

DAAT
METATRON

HOKHMAH

POWER

BEAUTY
Compassion, Harmony
Blessed, Holy One, King

GRACE

GEVURAH
♂

HESED
♃

TIFFERET
MICHA-EL
☉

SPLENDOR
Prophecy

ETERNITY
Prophecy

HOD
RAPHA-EL
☿

NETZACH
URI-EL
♀

FOUNDATION
Righteous One
Covenant, Phallus

YESOD
GABRI-EL
☽

PRESENCE (MALKOOT)
Kingdom, Queen, Communion of Israel
Apple Orchard, Vagina

SHEKHINAH
⊕

Mariam moved her hand to a place just below his navel. She sensed that Yeshua was still tense and pushed him on to his back while laughing she took hold of the visible proof of his tenseness:

'Get up, take up your bed and walk, you are healed.'

This was the sentence, which the itinerant healers used when they were healing the sick.

Her catching laughter finally made him let go. He wanted to embrace her, but she evaded him and returned to her task. Her hand with the ring circled in soft movements above the holy spot just below his navel. The cat also settled down and purred in Mariam's lap.

'Who are you?' he asked and put a hand on her hip.

'Hush! You'll know soon enough. All you have to do right now is to let go and listen.'

She pushed him back once more:

'Ten years ago I heard Helen of Tyre speak to a group of travellers in a small town on the coast down south. Her words cast a spell over all of us. But some of the men who were present got so agitated by her words that they wanted to stone her. Luckily she got away quite miraculously. People claimed at the time that she was a prostitute whom Simon the Magus had found in a brothel in Tyre.'

Yeshua once more wanted to say something but again she put a finger to his lips.

'Simon and Helen travelled together and spoke to the people and healed the sick. I once saw them in Alexandria. I have never seen two people so much in harmony with each other. They were like one. I have felt a strong closeness to her ever since I heard her for the first time. She was also educated by the Therapists at Mareotis outside Alexandria. Her way is a mirror of my own. She is the one who prepares the way.'

Now Yeshua interrupted:

211

'I once knew this Simon the Magus. Both of us were with the brothers at Carmel. He was the candidate of the Samaria brothers. For a while we were like brothers he and I. Of the two of us, he was the clever one. We separated when I went on my journey to the East. People now say that he has stooped to all kinds of magic and witchcraft.'

'That is the talk of evil tongues. He also prepares the way for that which is coming. And he has been baptized by Yohannan at Jordan.'

'What is it that is coming?' Yeshua asked.

He sensed that what she was talking about was something other than the expectations with which he had been brought up.

'Hush!'

She once more pushed him back on to the bed and continued the ritual.

'The image of Simon and Helen is an image of the most outstanding amalgamation. I now place that in your holy centre.'

She once more placed her hand on the spot below his navel, bending over him and kissing him. Then she whispered:

'I am *Shekhina,* the way, the truth and the life. *I am the silver cup from the tribe of Benjamin.'*

She got halfway up, swung her knee across him and straddled him like that. She then gently took hold of his member and moved it so that it touched her vulva.

'This is the Gate of *Shekhina.* This is the entrance to the wisdom you seek in vain in the scriptures. The words there are only shadows of what I'm going to show you now. The court of this temple represents *Yod, The Gate of Wisdom.'*

She slowly slid down over his member and stayed like that, immovably. He caught his breath and firmly held her hips, fighting with the power which wanted her to embrace him totally. From far away he heard her whispering voice:

'This is *He*, the *point of acknowledgement*. This is where you must stay until you have acknowledged your real goal and the cause behind your search. Only the true human being will resist giving in to the desire of the moment, because he knows that it is this desire that leads to his death.'

They stayed in this position for a long time. Yeshua looked at his beloved with half-closed eyes and saw her sitting upright in a state of trance with beads of sweat all over her body. Never before had he seen such a beautiful and noble being. For a long time Mariam was ready to give up. She was almost paralysed by the pain from the uncomfortable position, but before giving in to this weakness she floated into a state of openness where there was no room for pain. She was the dove, which had once been sent out from Noah's Ark to find new land. She had now found a wind which could carry her, and she floated about in the void all by herself.

Yeshua looked at her and couldn't resist the temptation to caress her breasts. His touch sent small shocks through her. It felt like a distress call through the universe and she immediately recognized the voice of the distressed one. She then circled the empty space and returned to the Ark.

For a fraction of a second she saw the being hidden in the man lying below her, waiting for her to lift him out of the darkness. They looked into each other's eyes. Two souls travelling through the universes, two souls reaching for the fruit of perfection. The fruit on the Tree of Knowledge in the Garden of Creation, waiting to be picked. She then took pity on him. Slowly, very slowly she slid down on him again until he was halfway inside her. The movement to this new position sent fire through both of them and pushed them dangerously close to the edge of the void from which Mariam had just returned.

'This is *Vav*, the *Gate of Grace and Compassion*,' she whispered.

Her breath was hot and intense. Yeshua sensed that she also was stepping across a new threshold.

'The one who may dwell here and keep his balance, shall finally be able to transform any kind of desire into pure love, the only desire being to give himself totally and unconditionally.'

He felt faint, but just before falling, he sensed how her words carried him and kept him floating in this inexplicable universe. He was losing his hold on her but clung to the seducing smell of aloe, myrrh, lovemaking and cinnamon. He lay completely still, afraid of losing his mind, mesmerized by her firm, joyous hold.

Where could she be?

He looked at her and tried to catch her eye but she looked right through him and into God knows what kind of reality. And as he lay there in this inexplicable state of mind, bound and yet free, he suddenly felt how feelings grew out from an unknown darkness, filling him with a kind of love which only wished to caress her, hold her and kiss her, and to be united with her eternally, because in her he recognized all life. In her he experienced the Universe. In her he saw his own best qualities expressed. Never, ever had he felt anything like this. The love that welled from his heart, so unconditionally, was the most vulnerable and the most powerful feeling he had ever had. It was limitless, excluding no one, embracing everything. With this he could perform miracles.

Barely had he experienced this new and wonderful state of mind than she slipped down on him and embraced him totally in a perfect unification. Words of blessing flowed through them:

'This is He, Shekhina, the Holiest of the Temple, the Heavenly Bridal Chamber. This is the place without a beginning and without an end. When the groom enters the bridal chamber he is anointed as Melchizedek reborn. Melchizedek is the King of Righteousness. He is Messiah, the Anointed One. She is Shekhina, the Heavenly Bride. Together they are the True Human Being, God's child.'

Then they let go and disappeared into each other. Here Yeshua saw all his shadowy sides: the conflict between the world of senses and his rigid, idealized version of heavenly life. The eternal endeavour for the pure and the elated at the cost of the defiled and the human. The fear of sensual and emotional needs. The anger and the wilfulness hidden behind the image of the altruistic and devoted saviour. The envy and the inferiority complex, the arrogance, the indignation and the assertiveness, which could make him hopelessly depressed, and the almost exhibitionistic self-centredness which saw himself as the Messiah. He now saw and recognized these shadows and understood that it was not helpful to repress them. Thus he set a power free which had been bound until now, a power filled with healing qualities, now uniting with its female counterpart: that unconditional gentleness and caring. Mariam witnessed the transformation of Yeshua because it took place in herself. It was through her that light was shed on his shadows, and thus they were awakened. Now she herself was able to transform and let go of all the reservations and prejudices that she had had towards him. Then they could merge into one being.

'That is the story of Mariam of Bethany,' said Mariam when she later told Yeshua everything that had happened to her during the years of separation.

'Now tell me your story.'

Yeshua sat up.

'At ten years old I was accepted by the Brotherhood on Mount Carmel. This is where I met Simon, the one who is now called the Magus. He had extraordinary powers already then. We were brothers in spirit. He was the preferred candidate of the older brothers in the beginning. But some of the other brothers had another candidate. That was me. This created a division, which then led to the decision to unite the tribes of the two great patriarchs, Benjamin and Judah. That is why you and I were betrothed at that time. Immediately after that I travelled to Alexandria where I studied the scriptures and languages as well as physics, metaphysics and astrology. I learnt about the body's properties and fluids and their effects, about the number of limbs and bones, vessels, arteries and nerves, about the correct mixture of warmth and cold and moisture and what followed from that, and the effect of the soul on the body, its feelings and abilities, about the ability to speak, to get angry, desires, and finally the ability to combine and judge as well as many other things. After three years I got the opportunity to travel to the East. In India I met a sage called Vidyapati. This was a major turning point for me. He told me about the way that was mine, but also that it was going to be hard to follow, because the people around me did not understand its real goal. He also told me that the time would come when I would attract much attention externally while I would be very unhappy internally because I was not understood. It was Vidyapati who prophesied that the help I needed would manifest itself when I needed it the most.'

He embraced her and held her close.

'And I must say that he was right.'

Shortly after, he continued his story:

'Returning from my travels almost four months ago, I soon learned that there was disagreement between the various

Mandean bride and groom of modern Iraq

factions of the Brotherhood and I therefore decided to come to this lonely place in order to think about my situation. I was here approached by some of the applicants whom I knew from my days on Mount Carmel and in Alexandria. This is how the whole travelling zoo came about. It reminds me of a Roman circus. It is in many ways a sad story. I'm on one mission, and most of my supporters are on another. In the course of these last months I have prayed that there would be just one person who would understand. And now here you are.'

Mariam and Yeshua stayed in the house in the abandoned village for seven days. Each day offered yet another initiation. In the course of seven days Mariam had shown Yeshua the possibilities which are latent in every human being, but which are more easily released through the holy union with the opposite sex. After seven days he was freed from all his shadows. Each of his seven centres had been cleansed and healed. All that was left was the final shared initiation.

On the morning of the eighth day Yeshua asked two of his disciples to come to him, Petrus and Yohannan. Petrus' natural distrust of women made him hesitant and morose. But it was obvious that Yeshua had undergone a considerable change, and he had to admit that. A new power radiated from him. It was a totally different man standing in front of them, than the one who had been sitting with them, resigned, closed and silent eight days ago, and who hadn't been able to make up his mind about anything. But Petrus didn't like the fact that this woman, apparently had, as if it was the most natural thing, taken the position which was rightfully his. But that's what women were like. They could turn a man's head just like that. That's what made them so dangerous. And that smile. How dared she? Was she mocking him?

'Prepare to leave. In three days there will be a feast in Cana.'

This command of Yeshua's spread like fire. Cana was the town where the rabbis from Carmel married, according to tradition. Cana was situated in the heart of Galilee. Therefore, there was no misunderstanding this invitation. Yeshua was going to get married. And there wasn't much doubt about the bride to be.

When the good news reached Yeshua's mother, Mariyam, she felt relieved. The only flaw in her happiness was the fact that the party had to be prepared in such haste that the usual preparations were not possible. It had been clear from the moment the original pact had been made that it was not going to be a common wedding. However, only the closest family had known the true purpose behind the reunion of the two tribes. At the time, an event had been planned that would surpass anything which had been seen before. That is why it took her by surprise that her son apparently had other plans. This did not promise well. Perhaps this Mariam of Bethany was not the one she had hoped for, after all. And what was that, arriving like that out of the blue, without informing her first? After all, she was the mother of the groom, and the only one of his parents who was still alive.

Cana was full of expectant people who had come from afar in order to attend the coming event. When a rabbi married it meant that he took full responsibility, not just as a holy man but also as a breadwinner. Most of the people were aware that this wedding would have quite another purpose for a man like Yeshua. But the precepts had to be kept. Yeshua's mother had relatives in the town. They provided a house for the bride and a couple of girls as helpers. On the wedding day the house had been decorated inside and out with oil lamps, so that it was obvious to everybody that this was where the bride was living. Mariam's sisters, Martha and Mari, and her brother Lazarus had arrived in time and had brought with them their mother's tiara and the dress which had been sewn for the wedding, at the time when it was supposed to have taken place. Now Mariam looked at both items and realized that neither the valuable tiara nor the artistically made gown had anything to do with the wedding pact she was about to accept. To the dismay of her sisters she declined to wear both the tiara and the dress. If she couldn't stand next to her beloved one in her white gown, she was not going to stand there at all. That was why both the helpers and her sisters were busy washing the linen and binding flowers.

Thus, everything was ready when the groom and his disciples and brothers came walking through the streets, carrying torches in their hands, in order to collect the bride of his choice and to ask the head of the family for her hand in marriage.

But when Yeshua arrived at the house of the bride he saw that there would be no asking for her hand in marriage since Mariam was standing in the doorway, waiting for him, radiating and ready, as he had never seen her before. The white gown shone bright with the most fantastic colours. The men around him went silent when they saw this being who had to come from another world. Yeshua reached out towards her and she took his hand and held it in hers. They stood close together. Then they walked hand in hand through the streets to the house of the groom.

One of the oldest men from Carmel had been called in to perform the ceremony. It was a solemn moment, which many had waited for. Now it was happening and those who attended cried because an old prophecy had come true. The married couple stood face to face looking into each others' eyes, and for the first time Yeshua saw the being whom he had just married. A being of inner beauty who could never be matched by an external form, except perhaps by the woman before him who must be the incarnation of the most perfect human. He now heard her voice, but was not sure whether it really was her talking or if it was his own voice. He heard her saying:

'Today we shall dress in our star body, the multicoloured emerald gown. Today, as one being once and for all, we shall abolish the limitation of matter. Today we shall transform all things dead into living water and cleansing fire.'

Then they melted into each other in a kiss while the crowd of people sang and cheered.

There were so many guests at the wedding party that they ran out of wine in the middle of the evening. The waiter was desperate when he informed Yeshua of the situation. Yeshua was about to tell the guests he regretted the lack of wine when Mariam said to the waiter:

'Wait. There is no cause for panic. Ask the waiter to fill the vats with water and let my beloved taste it before it is served.'

The poor waiter got even more nervous at this message. But Yeshua woke him from his stupor:

'Do as you are told!'

The waiter came back shortly after and handed Yeshua a goblet, beaming with joy:

'A miracle. Everybody usually serves the good wine at the beginning, and when the guests are quite drunk they put the bad wine on the table, but you do it the other way round.'

Yeshua smelled the delicious drink. He then turned to Mariam and said with a knowing smile:

'A miracle? Perhaps.'

He lifted his goblet, still holding Mariam's hand. Then he turned to his guests who had just heard of the miracle:

'Let this be a sign. Today, my bride and I are one.'

13

The trip to Syria was a turning point for me. Meeting the sisters of the Saydnaya Nunnery and Myrna in Soufanieh was a personal meeting with that aspect of the Mary archetype which is so wonderfully expressed in the collectivity of our day and age. Like thousands of people all over the world I had also been touched by the immediacy and implicitness of the revelations of Mary, which seemed to take place more and more wherever those of faith would meet. After returning home I became increasingly interested in how Mary Magdalene, as bearer of another aspect of the archetype, was linked to what might be called the superior aspect of Mary. I decided to return to Montségur in order to find an answer.

The Seer met me at the station in Foix, the town which was synonymous with arrivals and farewells. In spite of the fact that it was November the weather was fine and crisp. He drove me to the service station just outside the town where I had rented a car. We then, almost symbolically, drove our separate cars back to the house in town, which I now regarded as my second home. All the world may be out of joint, but when I pass the last hilltop before Mount Montségur and start the descent into the valley with the old village, my problems fade away. This to me is an earthly Shangri-La. Here time does not rule. Peace does.

The Seer and I had travelled far together. We had met many times throughout time, in other lives and other universes. Not just as Kansbar and Flegetanis, but in many other shapes without any names. We still had unsolved questions between us, something essential which we did not have the strength to touch this time round? Nevertheless, we were on the verge of a new version of our meeting in this life and we moved around ourselves and each other more or less clumsily, because both of us found it difficult to open up to the indescribable last barrier between us – *the new feminine force* – perhaps because it is not one-sided but unlimited in its expression.

The house received us with its familiar creaks and we carried our luggage to our rooms. Mona Lisa and Leonardo were still smiling at me from the wall like question marks as I moved into my usual room with the flowered wallpaper. We drank a single glass of red wine in the kitchen. The Seer seemed restless. Then he said:

'I'll take a walk on the mountain.'

The words were dry and it was a statement, which did not contain an invitation for me to join him. I was not surprised. I was conscious of the fact that the new reality we were entering contained a new way of working. I stayed home instead, and continued writing the book about Mariam. The Seer left. He came back half an hour later.

'She isn't there any more.'

The voice of the Seer was almost unrecognizable:

'Prat isn't there any more. It was very strange, but when I got to the usual spot she didn't show herself the way she usually does. I thought that maybe she was just playing, but I finally realized that she has gone.'

He poured himself half a glass of red wine. It was clear that he was, if not shaken, at any rate more than surprised.

We decided to drive around for a while, but didn't succeed in coming any closer to an explanation of this mystery. We went to bed early.

Before turning off the light I lay looking at a map of Montségur and the area. There was no particular reason for this. I wasn't looking for anything specific. But apparently my subconscious was, because suddenly a name on the map jumped out at me: *Roquefixade*. It was a town with a mountain and a castle, just like Montségur. There were only a dozen kilometres between the two places. Each time we had driven towards Montségur we had passed a sign to this place. But for some reason Roquefixade was the only Cathar castle we didn't take the trouble to visit. Now, suddenly, it was the only name that I noticed.

During the night I again moved about in the astral realms, but I was still unable to find Miriam, my oracle.

We had breakfast in silence. It was clear that the Seer was also struggling with something of his own. I was thinking about the event of the previous evening. Although I didn't feel like telling the Seer about it I nevertheless asked him if he would like to visit Roquefixade. He hesitated, but then answered a bit vaguely that he wanted to find a place where he could play some golf. We parted after breakfast and took off in our separate directions.

The landscape opened up in all its splendour when I entered the valley at the foot of Roquefixade. In contrast to

Montségur this town is built on a ridge. The mountain itself is above the ridge where the castle is situated. The surroundings here are also much more dramatic. Where Montségur is rounded, soft and open, Roquefixade seems more angular, hard and closed. I turned off and followed the narrow road winding its way towards my destination. Nobody was about.

When I arrived in the town it was bathed in sunshine while the castle higher up was almost hidden behind fog-like clouds. Suddenly the sun disappeared behind a cloud leaving the town embraced in the fog. I parked the car and tried to get an idea of the haphazard web of narrow streets and culs-de-sac. It was a charming town with a large square, and the surrounding houses looked like film-set buildings with nothing behind them. I walked about aimlessly, found the road leading to the mountain and decided to follow it. The dramatic impression it had given me to begin with proved to be correct. The road was close to the rock wall where the sheer cliff stretched towards the sky, discouraging and impregnable. Unlike Montségur there were no other visitors here but me. This was no tourist attraction but rather a personal challenge that had been waiting for me to take seriously.

The road split into two narrow paths. One seemed to continue around the mountain while the other apparently went directly to the castle. I turned off and followed the latter. Soon the path dissolved into mud and then nothing, and it was with the utmost difficulty that I continued to ascend. Further up I caught sight of something looking like another narrow path leading out between ragged rocks. I stepped between two large rocks forming a kind of gate through which I had to pass. The path now became even more dangerous. No mitigating circumstances here, just a look into a poorly defined abyss. There was just room to walk right on the edge. The fog was now so dense that I could only see about five metres ahead. After ten minutes of climbing, clinging to the cliff wall, I saw two ominous figures ahead of me. I stood rooted to the spot. After a while I tried to call out to them, but I received no answer. I then started moving forward again until I could see what was up ahead. Two large mountain goats stood in front of me with their horns lowered, looking very threatening. Behind them I could see the castle through a gap in the fog. Within me a voice broke through. The Voice which I had not heard for a long time.

'*This place is the manifestation of your repressions. Your decision to come here stems from the insight for which you are finally willing to take responsibility. However, as you see, there are things you were unaware of before you climbed up here. There are still some insurmountable obstacles that you must relate to if you don't want to fall into the abyss.*'

The Voice disappeared and I realized that I had to crawl back again. When I returned to the car and went to check the time, I discovered that my watch had stopped. When I tried to wind it the screw fell to the ground and I understood that maybe time – the old kind of time – was literally no more. I took off my watch and threw it into a field knowing that there was no going back. I was on my own.

Back in Montségur the Seer was waiting for me with a much-needed glass of red wine. I told him about my experience with the two mountain goats and my watch stopping. I could see something was waking in him.

'Let's go there tomorrow. We crossed the borderline where chance ruled long ago. It is time to face the consequences.'

It was my birthday the following day and I rose to a beautiful breakfast table prepared by the Seer. Later on we drove to

Roquefixade. After a walk in the town we started the ascent. In contrast to the previous day the mountain seemed more open. It was obvious that this mountain did not 'belong' to the Seer, but I could not help combining his presence with this openness. As usual, he went into the unknown without hesitation or reservation. We ascended the mountain without any difficulty. The mountain goats were nowhere to be seen and after 20 minutes of climbing we reached the plateau with the castle in front of us. The valley spread out as far as one could see. The Seer walked about for a while until he found a spot where he took up his usual pose. I walked into the castle. It had more rooms and split levels than its sister a dozen kilometres away. Standing at the top I spotted it, proudly looming on the horizon: Montségur. It was very strange, but I had never been aware that Roquefixade must also be visible from Montségur. They were the only two Cathar castles with a direct view of each other. I was wondering if it was significant and symbolic that one of the castles clearly represented the feminine aspect while the other just as clearly represented the masculine. The Seer joined me shortly after.

'This place is one of the fixed points of the universe. It belongs to the Brotherhood, while Montségur belongs to the Sisterhood.'

I immediately understood that the two spots were mutually dependent and that one could not be without the other.

'This castle may be the universe's gift to you.'

It was obvious that he was as moved by all this as I was. I, of course, was aware that this gift was purely symbolic and that it was about a specific question: did the chance of being healed have something to do with the unification of the two poles?

'Let's go to Montségur,' the Seer said and started the descent.

We arrived at Prat's meadow half an hour later. To our great surprise she was back at her usual place. She welcomed us in her usual kind way and asked us to be conscious of the climb we were about to make. Deep inside me I heard the Voice commenting on Prat's blessing:

'The heights to which this climb will take you are in direct ratio to the depths to which you have the courage to delve.'

Everything seemed clearer. The air was like a living crystal; lively beings of light danced around us. In front of us was the mountain, which had moved us more than any other reality we had experienced. We did not talk much but were on our way into a state of mind, which can only be described with a single word: acceptance.

On the way up we stopped at the various oracle points and, in the spirit of the day, the Seer stepped aside in order to let me be the first one to make contact. I received the answers as fast as I could ask the questions. There was no resistance. Everything flowed effortlessly in a manner that was so embracing that nothing was left out and everything was included, in the same way as everything found its rightful place.

When we stepped into the courtyard there was no doubt left in our minds. The Seer waited until I had stepped through the gate. Without hesitating I found the centre and drew a circle. The Seer was watching me from a distance with an expectant smile on his face. Within the circle I drew the star of Mariam. I then turned to him and invited him into the circle. He hesitated.

'It is your circle,' he said in a subdued way.

His whole attitude expressed a kind respect I had never experienced from him before.

Mandorla
(B Pinturicchio, 1550)

'I would be honoured if you would be the first one to step into it,' I replied.

I had never seen him more handsome or more in accord with himself and his destiny. I had never seen him more united with everything. Then he stepped into the circle, standing with his hands behind him, as a guest would do, while he nodded encouragingly and in acknowledgement. At this moment I understood that the Seer was not just one single person but in many ways also a projection. At this moment he was a projection of everything that I myself had not had the courage to express. I suddenly realized that the Seer was an idea and a state of mind. A state of mind which is open to all, when time and the specific student are ready for it. At that beautiful moment I saw how this man, five years earlier, had opened the door behind which I had barricaded myself, and had then lured me into the open so that my own hidden qualities could begin to react. We were now looking at each other here, perhaps at the end of the road. I hardly dared think. Then he stepped out of the circle again and signalled that I should take over and continue.

No sooner said than done. I stepped into it and found the centre of the star of Mariam. The Seer was standing at my right where I used to stand. Then he took a step away from the circle. With this gesture he wanted to make it clear that this moment was mine. I stood there with my eyes half closed feeling how the activity around me intensified. Two radiating circles appeared in the air in front of me. Slowly they met and touched. At that moment the light became more intense. Slowly the circles moved across each other until they formed a mandorla. Then I heard the Voice:

'This is the true healing of everything which until now has been divided. This is the true restoration of everything, which has been broken down. This is the end of all contrasts. This is the

231

gate of true rebirth through which all new life must pass, totally united.'

A mandorla, also called the *vesica piscis*, is the almond shape that appears when two circles overlap. It represents the female sexual organ, is found in the star of Mariam and is a divine symbol for the new, healing feminine strength. All true art is born through the mandorla. It is the birthplace of poetry and the preferred playground of the Muses. It is the end of all diseases and the only healing of hopelessness. It leaves nothing out and embraces everything. Through the mandorla everything repressed is made conscious and is transformed into clarity in the present.

*

Mariam sat looking across the vineyard, which had once been her father's pride. Now the fields lay fallow almost as a symbol of the destiny, which had befallen all of them. Her thoughts went back to the wedding and the happy times that followed. Together they had travelled all over the country. Yeshua had spoken to the people about the secrets that no one else wanted to introduce them to. Together they had healed the sick and raised the dead. At the beginning the disciples had shown their unconcealed dissatisfaction with these developments, but they slowly got caught up in the results of the healing sessions, and finally they themselves had begun laying their hands on people and raising the sick. Yeshua's mother joined them, and wherever they came they attracted huge crowds of people. They got more and more followers and little by little it became almost impossible for them to travel unnoticed.

It was far too late when Mariam noticed the dissatisfaction among the disciples. When Petrus and the others realized that the Kingdom of which Yeshua spoke, was not of this world, they became insecure and secretly started plotting. The golden future that Petrus had hoped for crumbled in front of him as over and over again Yeshua made clear that the enemy was not Caesar in Rome, but Caesar inside each one of us. Time and again Yeshua tried to make this point, but only Yohannan understood the parables through which Yeshua communicated the secret knowledge.

From the beginning Petrus had grasped at any opportunity to show his contempt for Mariam. This had spread to the other brothers who became confused about the fact that a woman not only possessed such knowledge but, far worse, that she was much wiser than they were. It was very difficult for them to see that a woman who ought to know her place in reality was the real centre from which the Power was flowing and who influenced their rabbi in a direction they did not understand. It was totally incomprehensible to them that in spite of the support of the masses, they did not care at all about worldly affairs, the power and the throne of Israel. What was the point of all their efforts? It didn't help that Yeshua and Mariam seemed to withdraw into solitude more and more frequently. When Petrus, the spokesman for the disciples, complained to Yeshua about all this, he was simply dismissed with a reprimand about his spiritual blindness and lack of faith.

Mariam should have seen it coming, but she had been so focused on her work that it was far too late by the time she realized what was going on. If she had known that Petrus and others used every opportunity, during Yeshua's healing and teaching sessions, to spread the news that he was to assume power as rightful king of the Jews she could have warned him so that they might take precautions. Instead, the rumours had reached Jerusalem and the new Governor, Pilate, who had sent out his spies to keep an eye on the rebels.

Finally there had been a direct confrontation. Petrus could no longer contain his rage. Self-righteously he claimed that he had been the one who made Yeshua's position possible. Had he not supported Yeshua right from the beginning? Now Yeshua must make up his mind. Would he assume responsibility for seizing power when the time was right? Or would he just carry on with his subversive activities that had no future and would certainly result in making a laughing stock of them all? Petrus was sick and tired of putting his energy into a mission that was leading nowhere. They all had families to support and there was a limit to how far this madness could go. Had he, Petrus, not been promised a seat to the right of the throne? Time was running out.

Yeshua had tried to calm Petrus and the other disciples down, but peace reigned for a short time only. The pressure on Yeshua grew. At the same time as he and Mariam continued their work, teaching and healing people, Petrus and his co-conspirators intensified the spreading of their message of the coming armed rebellion against Rome and the appointment of Yeshua as the true king of Israel.

The result of this propaganda was inevitable. Pilate's spies reported daily on the apparently innocent mission of Yeshua. But information that, under cover of this mission, a future uprising was being planned, made Pilate finally lose his patience and take necessary precautions.

The day Yeshua rode into Jerusalem on a donkey while, under pressure from Petrus and his followers, he allowed himself to be welcomed as a king, plans for his arrest were already on Pilate's table.

Mariam had tried to warn Yeshua but he believed right to the end that his disciples would understand and that it would be in his power to make them give up their plans for worldly power and dominion.

Yeshua was seized in the garden on the Mount of Olives the day after his entry into Jerusalem. Petrus and the others had protested loudly but were quickly scared away by the Roman detachment which, armed to the teeth, took Yeshua away. Mariam was the only one who followed him until she was turned away at the gate of Pilate's palace. Petrus and the other disciples fled and scattered to the four winds.

Mariam got up from the Syrian chair from which her father, in his day, had managed his affairs with a just hand. From the window she looked across the fields to the horizon as if she waited for someone. She had tears in her eyes. Thinking about these last days opened a sorrow that could never end. The most terrible thing had happened. Pilate had gone against the will of the people. He wanted once and for all to set an example to these militant religious fanatics, whom he did not understand, and whom he did not want to understand. The crucifixion of Yeshua had gathered a huge crowd. The disciples were nowhere to be found and there had been no rebellion. Instead, she had sensed that a major part of the priesthood in Jerusalem were not sorry at all that this had been the outcome. The candidate had been too controversial as it were.

She dried her eyes and shivered, thinking about the struggle going on in Jerusalem at the moment. Rumour had it that Petrus had found the only suitable successor to the throne: Yacob, Yeshua's brother, who had happily taken on the responsibility that Yeshua had denied himself. Petrus had been appointed High Priest and all the disciples held high positions in the new *Nazarene Church*. Mariam had heard terrible stories of how the true teachings had been twisted and instead had been used to affirm the position of the chosen ones. They also said that those who had supported Yeshua to the end were now persecuted and either driven from their homes or stoned to death. All had to stay in hiding. Yeshua's mother had gone to Antioch, accompanied by Yohannan, the most loyal disciple of Yeshua. Mariam's days in this country were also coming to an end.

The image of her beloved hanging on that terrible cross kept haunting her. She relived the painful hours in her mind when he struggled with himself, and the destiny he had taken upon himself. She had stayed with him to the end and had given him all her strength until he finally let go and passed to the other side. One of their faithful followers, Yoasaph Arimataeus, had placed his own tomb at their disposal, and Mariam for the third time had anointed Yeshua in accordance with the old secret laws which she had been taught, so that the finer bodies of light would be able to let go of the physical and, if possible, dissolve his mortal frame.

She had gone to the grave three days later. She had rolled the entrance stone of the tomb aside with the help of two male Therapists. Once in the tomb, they saw that the miracle had happened. Mariam's efforts had paid off, Yeshua was gone. Only the shroud was left. Mariam held it up and thought she could see the image of his face and the outline of his body printed on the fine white material. She then kissed the shroud, folded it carefully and prepared to leave the tomb. But then it happened that she felt his presence. A faint pulsating outline of him suddenly became visible in the dark tomb. She wanted to reach for him, but before she managed that, she heard his voice inside herself:

'Do not touch me. I am still in my other being. Be patient. Rukha d'koodsha is with you. We shall always be together in my SHM.'

236

After this experience, she then visited Petrus and the disciples for the last time in the hope that she would be able to initiate them into the true teaching. But they just scorned her and threw her out. She had fled under cover of darkness and barely escaped their pent-up bitter anger.

Now she was looking at the cloud of dust, which slowly approached Bethany from the horizon. She went below in order to prepare herself for the journey. Soon after two men came riding into the courtyard.

The following day they put out to sea from the harbour of Joppe. She stayed at the rail for a long time watching the white coastline evaporating into the blue. She then looked ahead. In the air in front of her she saw a transparent radiating and deeply purple ball with a pink four-pointed star, surrounded by a thin pink line. Somewhere out there Gaul was waiting for her. Somewhere out there a new life was waiting for her.

It was a moving moment. The Seer was my witness – and I was his. We left the circle intact in the middle of the castle and started the descent. We didn't speak but slipped into the contemplative state of mind that both of us knew so well and which didn't crave any explanation because it was the closest we could get to an authentic mode of being.

*

I couldn't let go of the experience with the radiating mandorla. It was beyond any doubt that as a symbol it was related to the star of Mariam. But why did it appear now?

I have written quite a few things about the mandorla in one of my earlier books, *The Silence of the Heart*. Perhaps this archetypal figure had been waiting dormant in my subconscious for something to activate it at the right moment?

'Why don't you ask the universe?' the Seer suggested. 'You know that you must look at the problem from a higher perspective. And I have told you this so often, that you ought to know it by now. Ask yourself the question what has been the red thread through your work with Mariam.'

'The Kabbalah?'

'Exactly. Something must be hiding there that you haven't yet seen.'

The Seer's suggestion seemed sensible. It was time to take stock. In my work with Aramaic I, among other things, had come across the latest research on the Kabbalah. Until recently I didn't know that there was a Greek parallel called the Greek Kabbalah. Here a literary tool is used called the Gematria by which you may find the numerical, holy value of ideas and sentences. They do not have special symbols representing numerals in Aramaic or in Greek. They use the letters of the alphabet instead. That way you may find the root of an idea or a word, and by way of the Gematria see its position in relation to other holy numerals and terms in classic cosmology. I had read in a book on the subject that the old magi who practised the principles of Gematria used the number 153 to express the form that defines the mandorla. When you take the sum of the Greek idea of *h Magdalhnh* = Magdalene (in the definite, singular: that is not a Magdalene but *the* Magdalene) then the result would be 153. If this was not a coincidence it was probable that already in the first century AD certain traditions saw Mary Magdalene as the incarnation of a superior, feminine principle. The question then remained why she seemed to have played a significant role within Christianity?

As I have mentioned earlier in this book, there are no reliable sources supporting the idea that Mary Magdalene was a prostitute or specifically sinful. The town *Migdal,* which is supposed to be the source of her name, did not exist at the time of Yeshua. Furthermore, the tradition of giving people nicknames was not limited to the name of your home town. It was quite as common to give people a nickname relating to specific virtues, abilities or specific missions. Nicknames like *The Baptist* and *The Magus* speak for themselves. Even Yeshua's, *The Nazarene,* cannot be ascribed to the town of *Nazareth,* since that didn't exist at his time either. On the contrary, his name referred to the sect Yeshua was a member of, perhaps even its leader.

If we do take the meaning of the name Magdalene seriously, it tells us that the bearer of that name was considered to be the Spirit of the Exalted Peace. If her name is added up in the following manner: 1 + 5 + 3 you get 9. Nine is a triad times three. It is the figure denoting completion. It denotes the beginning and the end. It is unity. Nine melts opposites together. It unites fire and water. It is expressed in the mountain and the valley. It is symbolized by the sword and the cup. It is the Foundation Stone itself.

After the disappearance of Yeshua, Mariam also had to disappear. The Church which became the foundation for Hellenistic Christianity, to which we belong, had no room for a feminine expert who, apart from her direct access to the Power, was also able to act in life in harmony with the cosmic principles. They wanted to build a patriarchal order in which the female virtues such as self-sacrifice and compassion did not find their place till several centuries later through the idealized Virgin Mary.

The aspect of the Mary archetype represented by Mary Magdalene was literally thrown out. Her vision of the integrated, sensitive human being did not fit into the patriarchs' ideas about a holy life. That is why this aspect had to disappear.

Mariam Magdalene arrived in France bringing all her knowledge about the cosmic principles, which is partly to be found in the Kabbalah today. This knowledge was later hidden behind the term the Holy Grail. Perhaps because Mariam was the silver cup that, according to prophecies, the Messiah from the line of David would find in the tribe of Benjamin, a secret movement sprang up following her arrival in the south of France. One of the places it showed itself was among the Cathars and their female priestesses as well as through other esoteric underground movements from which the occult life in Europe has drawn invaluable spiritual sustenance. Mariam Magdalene was the true founder of esoteric Christianity.

The decision that Yeshua was the true Christ, a decision which was made at the first synod in the year 325, was made on the basis of very few, specifically chosen, gospel sources. The Yeshua in whom most Christians now profess to believe could very well be the result of a one-sided, collective focusing of energy, which has been invested in this specific interpretation of the life and work of Yeshua. This energy, with time, has been stored in the ethereal Akasha. The energy follows the thought. And it is our thoughts, that create the reality in which we find ourselves. Thus, the Gospels do not necessarily say anything about what really happened, but more about the need of people to trust in a saviour who will take their sins upon himself. Unfortunately, this is also the secret behind the sad condition of the world. Through the preservation of this comfortable idea it has been possible for us, at a deeper level and for centuries, to live and act without taking spiritual and moral responsibility for ourselves and the proverbial neighbour. In turn, through our idea of

Christ, we have created a force which is still effective and which manifests itself in the ethereal plane when called upon with sufficient intensity, in exactly the same way as the many revelations of the Virgin Mary, which are also the result of humanity's profound need for presence, care and love. In this century a new feminine force is showing itself, a force embracing the entire human being, both body and spirit. It is the force characterized by Mary Magdalene, which for example we have seen manifested in the twentieth-century feminist movement.

Mariam Magdalene is the manifestation of a new feminine form of energy coming down from above as *Rukha d'koodsha*, a feminine form of energy which is not limited to pure motherliness, the receptive and the neutral, which until now has been the hallmark of the universal feminine archetype.

This new form of energy has come into being as an opportunity for both men and women, because the old, patriarchal energy has had its day. This patriarchal energy has been a necessary activating factor, which, however, no longer manifests itself for the good of the human race, but solely for its own sake. It is separatist, divisive and egotistical, an earthly flame which is now dying.

The new power is inclusive, healing and altruistic. It is the carrier of the cosmic fire and the living water. It contains everything, both the masculine and the feminine, but it is more feminine than masculine.

In the evening I invited the Seer to a birthday dinner at the Le Castrum restaurant, where earlier he had shown some of the more intriguing aspects of his unique abilities. This time, however, he stayed in his chair during dinner, although he couldn't quite refrain from an innocent flirt with the young waitress.

Looking at him on top form, I once more entertained the thought that this might be the last time we met like this – as teacher and student. The thought made me sad because it indicated an end as well as the beginning of something new. The time had come to take up my bed and walk. In other words: the time had come for me to be responsible for myself. But, as usual, the natural modesty between us denied us the opportunity of touching on the subject. I therefore pushed the thoughts out of my mind and instead threw myself into the unbridled fun of the moment – together with a dear friend and itinerant miracle-maker. We were just two drops of water on our way to the sea of eternity.

After we had returned to the house and had gone to our own rooms, I lay on my bed looking into the eyes of Da Vinci smiling at me through the portrait of the Mona Lisa. It was as if he was smiling at those of us who didn't understand the simple truth expressed in his painting. The truth about the isogynic being. As a Grand Master of the old, esoteric order of the Priory of Sion, Da Vinci was well aware of the secret behind the work of Yeshua. If you study a number of his paintings you'll find that they are filled with signs and symbols, which literally point to quite a different interpretation of the individual importance of the central characters in the New Testament. John the Baptist especially plays a major part in Leonardo's interpretation, and the appearance of Mary Magdalene in *The Last Supper* is yet another example of his insight into the esoteric secrets.

I actually heard him laughing out loud in a voice that sounded in long-forgotten corridors of my subconscious mind:

'Why all the vain efforts? Let it go. Why make it more difficult than it is? Spirituality does not mean that you struggle along from one place to another but rather that you are open-minded and move within the eternal now. The integration of the relative and the absolute is always actualized outside of time and space. Each human being contains everything. EVERYTHING!

'Everything that you want to become, you already are. Wake up from the dream and realize that you are awake. Everything has meaning. Wake up and realize that each and every human being is the very image of God. Wake up to the eternal life. This is the truth about the parable of the mustard seed.'

The voice faded away and I moved through the spheres. Everything seemed much lighter than I had experienced it before. This meant that I didn't, at first, recognize the various universes. But suddenly, I was standing in the basement passage I had looked for so desperately and for such a long time.

I slowly floated through the passage towards a door behind which I hoped to find my oracle. I took hold of the handle and watched the door open. She was sitting on her cream-coloured leather couch with her legs pulled up, in absolute peace.

'Good you could come,' she said with a smile, 'I have been expecting you. Come and sit down. You must have a lot to tell me.'

She quietly patted the couch. I stepped inside.

I heard the door closing shut behind me.

I sat down beside her.

'Now, tell me,' she said impatiently.

I opened the manuscript and started reading.

It had been raining all that Sunday and also throughout the night. It was as if the floodgates of the Flood itself had been opened. I was in my study lost in the endless rain and the soaked landscape outside. The air was tense with static electricity. Something indefinable was gathering across the sea, a series of dark shadows of breaking clouds filled with unanswered questions.

I had just finished the manuscript for *Mary Magdalene*, when the phone rang . . .

In a time characterized by war and unrest, economic instability, religious extremism, global environmental problems and spiritual estrangement, His Holiness the Dalai Lama is travelling around the world with his simple message of inner peace and compassion. Whenever he visits the West, he urges all those brought up in the Christian faith to remain Christians and deepen themselves in the esoteric aspects of Jesus' teachings.

An increasing number of Christians, however, seek this esoteric wisdom in vain. Fortunately, there is now help at hand. In Lars Muhl's book, *The Law of Light*, one can, through the psychology underlying the Aramaic language, get an insight into Jesus' hidden wisdom, as expressed in the New Testament.

If not us, then who?

If not now, when?

Otherwise known as the Grail Trilogy, *The O Manuscript* includes *The Seer*, *The Magdalene* and *The Grail*. This is the compelling full account of Lars Muhl's spiritual awakening, written with extraordinary energy, candour and humility. It is a personal and philosophical quest that challenges conventional wisdom and takes the reader on a mystical journey through ancient history and modern times.

A work in three volumes, the book begins with the author at a crossroads, suffering from debilitated health, his personal and professional life disintegrating around him. Bedridden for three years, Lars Muhl was put in touch with a seer who helped him, over the telephone initially, to recover his energy and brought him back to life. The Seer became his spiritual leader, teaching him the inner truths of existence.

The second and third parts of the trilogy cover the Female principle, followed by that of the Bridal Chamber, a Sufi concept, in which both the Male and the Female meet to form One Unity. This trilogy is not only a spellbinding introduction to the ancient vision of cosmic interconnectedness, but also a critical evaluation of a long list of limiting New Age dogmas.